SALVAGED FROM THE FLOOD

BRIAN PAIGE

Paperback ISBN: 979-8-9894006-0-7
Hardcover ISBN: 979-8-9894006-1-4
E-Book ISBN: 979-8-9894006-2-1

Cover and inner photos by Brian Paige unless otherwise specified.

Printed in the United States of America

ACKNOWLEDGMENTS

I would like to take this occasion to thank a variety of people who mean so much to me: My wife, Amanda; son, Andrew; my mother, Phyllis; and my brother, Eric. I would also like to thank various friends for helping contribute to the various stories in this book, even if I felt the need to change names at times.

I would like to thank several teachers from Butler Traditional High School from my days there: Ron Orwick, Sherry Ederheimer, Dottie Ballard, and Martha Gutermuth. I have had many other teachers over the years, but these are the ones who believed in me and encouraged my writing.

I would also like to thank Jimmy Humphrey for his film help back in 2006 and also for readily reading and commenting on any piece I send his way. The same goes for Rachel Ingram, who I consider the sister I never had. Rachel is usually willing to read anything I have written and gives quality feedback.

Special thanks to Russell Womack and Brittani DiMare, the primary editors of the book. Special thanks to Arthur Fogartie for additional editing on *Beechmont,* as well as Rana Williamson for additional editing on *The Sub Par Filmmaker.*

CONTENTS

INTRODUCTION

I often think back to a particular Sunday in January 1994—the last day of winter break. My dad was about to start a new job at Byerly Ford, a car dealership in Shively, Kentucky, close to where I went to high school at Butler. That day was unique because it was the only time I have ever been to two movies at two different theaters, in two different states, on the same day. My family went across the Kennedy Bridge to River Falls Mall in Clarksville, Indiana, to see a matinee showing of *Tombstone*. Even my four-year-old brother, Eric, went with us.

After eating at Burger King on Preston Highway, my mom and Eric went home, but my dad and I went to the Showcase Cinemas on Bardstown Road to see *The Pelican Brief* for an evening showing. We had to do this since there wasn't going to be a better time to see both movies, and back then not every movie played at all theaters. At the time, I may have enjoyed *The Pelican Brief* more, but since then I have no doubt seen *Tombstone* about a hundred times. I hardly care about *The Pelican Brief* at all these days.

My dad never worried about taking us to see R-rated movies like *Tombstone*, though. When I was a kid, he took me to see *Rambo: First Blood Part 2*, *Robocop*, *Return of the Living Dead*, and any cheesy

Cannon Films action movie showing at Oxmoor Mall. If something in a movie upset Eric or me, we would discuss the scene on the way home. But my dad was a study in odd contrasts. A lifelong Democrat, he was an NRA member until 1994, when they became too looney for him.

Recently when I thought about that day, I realized nothing we did is even possible today. River Falls Mall is little more than Bass Pro Shops now with no theater, and the tolls on the Kennedy Bridge didn't exist then. The Showcase Cinemas closed in 2004, eventually replaced by a Costco. Even the Burger King closed some years ago. The changes don't stop there. I went to an elementary school, Gilmore Lane, which no longer exists. (Liberty High School moved into the building to make room for the new W. E. B. DuBois Academy). I spent summers at the now-defunct University of Louisville daycare near campus. Even a weekend afternoon spent in the Highlands shopping for records at Ear-X-Tacy and then going to Hawley-Cooke Bookstore is a thing of the past. Oxmoor Mall still exists, but the theater does not. The list is endless. Even most of the baseball card and comic shops I used to frequent are long gone.

Salvaged From the Flood was originally a series of poems and short stories I wrote in high school, pieces of writing I saved from the trash heap after we were flooded out of our apartment in March of 1997. While most of those writings do not need to see the light of day, the title itself remains. The cover photos feature the old, now vacant Holiday Inn (later Fern Valley Hotel) on Fern Valley Road, in front of where I used to live at Tanglewood Apartments. The apartment complex borders what used to be the Edgewood neighborhood, but the neighborhood too is gone. Now the area is used by UPS, eerily similar to the fate of the old Highland Park neighborhood my grandparents lived in at one time. Edgewood and Holiday Inn may be gone, but oddly enough, Tanglewood remains.

This book is not so much my entire life story as it is a series of narratives serving as snapshots of particular moments in time, of dreams and aspirations, as well as heartache and dreams deferred. Sometimes I skip around a few years if there isn't a fascinating story to tell, or if I can't find the words to tell it. This is the story of a diehard Louisvillian who badly wanted to escape Louisville, but as of this writing, never has found anywhere better. The first two chapters I wrote pertained to youth baseball, one being my own experiences at Beechmont and the other my son Andrew's experiences playing at Prairie Village. Those two chapters serve as bookends, starting in 1991 and ending in 2022.

While at various points I discuss baseball, my lifelong love of University of Louisville basketball, and even pro wrestling, this is not exactly a sports story. At various points, other topics take center stage, including screenwriting, filmmaking, cryptocurrency, or personal relationships through the years.

The chapters on my experiences with U of L debate as a graduate student function as a self-contained novella. Admittedly, the first chapter, "Rebels with a Cause," is a crash course on debate terminology and lingo but give it a chance. Events occurring in the first half of the story have payoffs in the second half. One debate chapter is amusingly titled "College Debate Is Decadent and Depraved" in tribute to fellow Louisvillian Hunter S. Thompson.

The major omission from the high school chapters would be my old German teacher, Ron Orwick. Since German class was a separate entity and few of my regular classmates were involved, talking at length about Mr. Orwick's class didn't come into play. He was and still is a fascinating man, a songwriter and musician in addition to a German and Algebra teacher. Perhaps there will be a time when I write that story, but it didn't fit anything in this book.

Life can be hilarious, frustrating, romantic, exhilarating, and heartbreaking. Hopefully, these emotions come through in various chapters of this book, sometimes several in close proximity. I don't know if people will identify with everything I have to say, but hopefully some aspects of my experiences will register. Life does not fit into any one genre, so why should a book?

PART ONE

WELCOME TO PARADISE

CHAPTER 1

BEECHMONT

"I have a World Series ring. You don't."

Those words stung. One of my son's youth baseball games at Prairie Village Babe Ruth League had gotten out of control, with the other team's first base coach arguing with my son's coach in addition to several parents. While sitting in the bleachers, I became fed up and felt the need to intervene.

"Shut up. You are acting like an idiot. Coach your own team and quit jaw jacking with other coaches and parents," I said. When he fired back with the ring comment, I didn't have a response. My son's team won the game 14-2, but I spent the rest of the night upset by this altercation.

I looked him up on the league app. I realized I had been arguing with Josh Robinson, a member of the 2002 Valley Sports team that had won the Little League World Series. I'd been quite proud of those kids and frankly a little jealous because I never had a chance at that level of All Star success. The 2002 Valley Sports team was a validation of a whole era of youth baseball in Louisville. I always viewed our area as a hotbed for youth baseball, but the politics in the leagues often put All Star success out of reach.

Dealing with such nonsense, as well as my son's current All Star candidacy, caused me to reflect on my own playing days at Beechmont, a league in Louisville's south end next to the old Naval Ordnance property. When I played, Beechmont was also adjacent to the Americana Apartments. Beechmont is a well-known league in Louisville, but to my knowledge has never had any postseason tournament success. I was a three-time All Star at Beechmont when I was nine, ten, and thirteen. You may wonder what happened when I was eleven and twelve, the age when players competed for things like the Little League/Babe Ruth World Series.

Except for one year, I played for Coach Larry Kirby at Beechmont, from the time I was seven until I was eleven. We were always a good team, but never won the league title. When I was seven, we reached the championship game but lost. The 1991 team might have been the best of the bunch. The roster was loaded with Rob Brewer (who now coaches at Prairie Village, my son's league), power hitting sluggers Robbie Wilson and Davey Pitt, the coach's son, Devin Kirby (who also pitched and was solid at most stuff), and, of course, me. I mainly played first base and was an excellent singles/doubles hitter.

Each team was allowed up to four All Stars for the 11–12 division. Nowadays they split teams into different ages and allow more players on All Star teams, but in the early '90s, it was four guys per team. Brewer, Wilson, and Pitt were no-brainer picks. In an ideal world of putting together the best team, the fourth pick would have been me, but in this case, I was competing with the coach's son for the final All Star selection, so I had no chance. I was the better player by a decent margin, but Devin wasn't a disgrace or anything.

The All Star team started practicing when our regular team was prepping for a playoff semifinal game. In our last practice at Iroquois High School, I can remember a frustrated Pitt ranting at the coaches, "Why is Brian not on the All Star team? Have you *seen* what we have at first base?"

Not only was I passed over, but the geniuses at Beechmont who put the team together hadn't selected a viable first baseman. This sort of thing was always Beechmont's problem in postseason tourneys. The league was more about political favors than putting together a quality team.

Making matters worse, the Kirbys divorced around that time and Devin's mom took him to Colorado for a skiing vacation, blowing off the All Star competition entirely. What I didn't understand at the time (and never will) was why they didn't add me to the team as an alternate. I have no idea if they played one man down or selected someone from another team. Regardless, it was a frustrating experience and I never played for Kirby again. In our big playoff game, we lost in the semis. I made the final out of the season by grounding out to second base, one of the low points of my playing days. Robbie Wilson's dad was our first base coach. He screamed at me during my entire at bat. I could barely focus.

In the weeks following the 1991 season, my maternal grandfather died. August 5th, a day seared into my memory. My grandparents were staying at their house near Nolin Lake. Grandpa had a heart attack during the night and never woke up. This was the first major loss I had ever experienced, and it affected me deeply. The funeral home in Clarkson had an old school Coca Cola machine, and I downed several bottles while I sat in the lobby—pretty much the main thing I remember about the service. My grandma sold the lake house and the boat in 1994. I asked if she would give me $10 from the sale, only being half serious. She gave me $100.

Coach Kirby stopped coaching at Beechmont soon after. Looking back, I don't understand the logic. He would have had the dominant favorite to win the title given most of the best players were eleven-year-olds and would have been back the next year. Since Coach quit, the team disbanded, and the talent was spread all over the league. Devin Kirby ended up on a mediocre team even though he was still an All Star. Pitt and Wilson suffered the same fate. I was the lucky one. I landed on Rick Lawler's Twins team for the 1992 season. (That season was the end of an era for all the twelve-year-old boys since the following year involved a huge leap of playing on the big field with its daunting ninety-foot baselines and a pitching rubber sixty feet, six-inches from the plate.)

We were okay in the first half of the season, as Steve Feist's Angels team, led by his son David, stormed out to an 8–1 record and clinched a playoff spot. We had a 6–3 record for the first half.

Lawler was the only coach I ever played for who maximized what I could do. I still played first base, but I also pitched more innings than anyone on the team, mainly in long relief. The best hitter on the team, and maybe the greatest hitter I've ever played with in any season, was Jacob Rogers. Jacob hit an absurd .569 with eleven home runs, staggering numbers. No one else on the team even had one home run, though I came close a couple of times. Oddly, I don't recall Jacob ever having such a season before or after 1992. He was the classic case of a guy who grew a bunch when he was twelve, but when everyone else caught up, his massive homers turned into deep fly balls on the big field.

The second half of the season we came to life and refused to lose a game, winning one crazy one-run contest after another. David Feist hurt his arm and missed several games and the Angels slumped to 5-4 in the second half, so we fought with Keith Schwartz's team for the spot in the playoff game versus the Angels. Schwartz's Yankees squad went 14-4 during the season but finished one game behind in both the first and second halves and barely missed the playoffs.

I ran into my old friend Jeremy Stigler at Tire Discounters recently. He was on the Yankees team, and he is *still* bitter about not making the playoffs that season, despite being tied for best overall record in the league. Jeremy, a big redheaded kid, was one of my closest friends both from our rivalry at Beechmont and our participation in the University of Louisville summer daycare program. He went to Butler High School as well in the Class of 1998. (I was Class of 1997.) For whatever reason, we drifted apart after we aged out of daycare.

I never had an argument or anything with Jeremy, but I tried calling him later in 1992; he didn't have time to talk, and I never bothered calling him again. When we met at the tire store, Jeremy drove home a notion I have had for quite a while now. For numerous men our age, youth baseball created a haunting sense of being unfulfilled accompanied by a certain amount of nostalgia.

Before the final game of the regular season, Rick Lawler pulled me into the batting cage area to have a talk. He told me I hadn't made the All Star team, despite doing everything for the team other than selling popcorn. The picks were going to be Rogers, Mike Lawler, and Jeff Lawler (both the coach's sons), and of all people, Tod Matthews. To this day, I still can't wrap my head around how Tod made All Stars over me. Tod was our main starting pitcher and decent enough, but I finished the games. Tod certainly was nowhere close to me as a hitter. He was my teammate the following year and we never talked about why he made All Stars and I didn't. I can assume his dad was tight with Lawler and had some deal in place guaranteeing Tod a spot, but I have no firm idea. We lost the meaningless regular season finale, snapping an eight-game winning streak.

We crushed a still ailing David Feist and Co., 11-2, in the playoff game, and then won the league championship the next day in a rubber match with Matt O'Riley and the Pirates, 8-5. I pitched the last three innings, the most nervous I had ever been on a baseball field. I escaped a bases loaded jam in the fifth inning and then retired the side in the sixth. I didn't need the All Star games. This was the mic drop, and the last time I would ever play at Beechmont. Given all the crazy one-run victories, I almost thought there was some sort of *Angels in the Outfield* intervention going on, like my grandfather was tipping the scales from above. For his part, Jeremy attended the championship game and rooted for my team to win, although I can't help but wonder if he felt his team should have been there instead.

The celebration was short-lived, however. Within a couple of weeks, my dad needed emergency surgery for diverticulitis and was laid up in the hospital for quite a while. He'd been misdiagnosed with a urinary tract infection. As such, I missed the team's postseason get-together. My time at U of L daycare ended as well since I had turned thirteen and aged out of the program. My dad eventually recovered, although the surgery left a serious scar on his stomach which needed to be bandaged for several months. The old U of L daycare closed some years later. It sat empty for a decade until it became the Stoddard Johnston Scholar House (apartments for single-parent students and their families).

One day I was home alone. Mom was at the hospital. There was a knock on the door. Rick Lawler had somehow found our address. He said he was sorry to hear about my dad and brought my trophy as well as a stats sheet of the team, which frankly interested me more than the trophy since this was the first team I had been a part of that kept detailed records.

After Lawler left, I put the trophy down in my room and scoured the stat sheet. As noted, Jacob Rogers was the hitting star. I finished second on the team at .424. Everyone else was in the .300 range or lower. I was 9-2 in pitching decisions, had the most innings pitched, and a 2.63 ERA, lowest on the team. If there had been a league MVP vote for the season, it would have almost certainly come down to Rogers and me. But again, I didn't make the All Star team. What kind of league doesn't put one of its two best players on the All Star team? Certainly not one interested in winning anything. Whatever I achieved in the 1992 season didn't matter to anyone, except me. Josh Robinson may well have peaked when he was twelve by being a part of the 2002 Valley Sports team, but even if he does nothing meaningful the rest of his life he always has that accolade to fall back on. Winning the 1992 championship at Beechmont still means the world to me, even if the average person could care less.

I could understand the situation with Kirby the previous year even if I didn't like it, but what happened with Lawler was a total breach of faith. I had the single greatest season of my life for Coach Lawler and didn't gain any recognition for it. Making things even weirder, Lawler kept coaching at Beechmont, but never picked me for his team again. I stopped trying to figure it out years ago. Only Miles Durham, who I played for at age ten and then later as a teen, was legit in terms of All

Star selections. When I was good enough to be an All Star for Durham, I made the team. When I wasn't, I did not.

The ironic aspect about bemoaning not being selected for All Stars was that I detested my experiences at Fern Creek in the 1989 and 1990 All Star tourneys. Even then, I knew Beechmont's teams were poorly constructed jokes riddled with politics, nepotism, cronyism, and coaches who didn't know the players well enough. I even performed well at these tournaments, but no matter what I did at Beechmont, no one ever cared.

So no, I don't have a Little League World Series ring. I never had any chance at one, although I seriously doubt my being on the Beechmont All Stars would have changed the outcome very much. There are no doubt hundreds of similar stories about Little League politics online. I imagine politics and a general lack of sportsmanship has harmed leagues around the country and helped give rise to the disaster known as travel team baseball. But that is a rant for another time.

In 2014, I subbed for Coach Lawler's eldest son, Greg, for a couple of days at Butler High. I left a note asking if his dad still remembered me from Beechmont, then the next time I subbed there I stopped by to talk to Greg.

"My dad absolutely remembers you. He said you were good. Real good."

"Just not good enough to make the 1992 All Stars at Beechmont," I replied. He stood there puzzled by my remark as I left the room.

CHAPTER 2

THE SEASON OF SOMMER

I started at Butler Traditional High School in August 1993. Butler was barely on my radar while I was in middle school other than occasionally practicing baseball there. Since I went to middle school at Noe, mainly due to Noe having advanced placement classes, the obvious path would have been to head right across the street to DuPont Manual High School. Manual is *the* public high school in Jefferson County, with a litany of Governors Scholars and multiple magnet programs (High School to University, Art, Math/Science/Technology, Journalism & Communications). I initially applied to HSU and was accepted.

There was trouble in paradise, however, as the administration at Manual got cold feet when someone took a closer look at my record at Noe. While my GPA was solid, I missed over a hundred days of school over those three years. I had constant sinus infections throughout middle school, but truth be told, I despised Noe with a passion reserved for no other school. I didn't care for my classmates. I didn't like the bizarre open section classes where bookcases separated various classes in lieu of actual walls. Realizing I had taken Mrs. Bannister's Performing Arts Class at Noe, Manual amended my offer from HSU acceptance to Youth Performing Arts School.

I transferred out of the PAC class midway through eighth grade. The class wasn't what I signed up for (originally a video class, which merged with Bannister's dance class). The idea of going to YPAS was a nonstarter, so I wound up missing my chance to go to Manual. Since my home school was Iroquois, one of the worst schools on earth, I desperately sought other options. My baseball coach at Beechmont, Miles Durham, suggested Butler. His oldest son, Brett, already attended, and while he mentioned Butler being a "traditional" school, he said the traditional aspect was no big deal. Wear blue jeans with a belt and otherwise things are similar to other schools. I was accepted to Butler easily enough. Principal Kenneth Frick told my dad I needed to improve my attendance, but otherwise I was good to go.

My first two years at Butler went well. Early on, the traditional aspects were limited to the always strange morning announcements ("Let's pause for a moment of silent meditation") and the slightly stricter dress code. Most of the bad behavior I dealt with at Noe was gone, and troublemakers were shown the door. As my junior year started, the administration at Butler went to a more formal dress code consisting largely of red, white, or navy-blue polo shirts, as well as khaki or navy-blue slacks. Overnight, the entire school looked like a group of pro golfers. My tenure was split in half: two years before the stricter dress code and two years after. Those in the Class of 1996, however, had to adjust to this for their senior year. The dress code wasn't an excuse for the antics I am about to describe, but I had more with other students in the wake of the stricter dress code being implemented.

The idea of being catfished wasn't much of a known concept back when I was in high school since it is more of an internet phenomenon. The internet was barely starting to become a thing during my high school years, with Butler being wired for student internet use for maybe the second half of my senior year in 1997. Before then? I didn't know much about the Net. That said, catfishing still occurred on a lo-fi level, and during my junior year of high school, it absolutely happened to me. The following tale is one of embarrassment and humiliation, although I will admit I played into things and kept the charade going.

11

The situation started with the crew I sat with at lunch, which included two Jims, Hitchens, and Nord, as well as a senior named Mick Logsdon. Hitchens was a reasonably good friend of mine in high school, even if I never cared for his right-wing politics. Nord was a tall, heavy-set guy and the single most misanthropic person I knew in high school. I don't know if I ever especially *liked* Jim Nord as a person since he made that all but impossible, but he was in a bunch of my classes and we talked often enough. For someone like me who struggled to make friends, I had to make do.

Mick Logsdon was a different matter. Logsdon, a senior, felt the need to hang around us juniors at lunch. I had taken Algebra 2 with Mick the prior year and found him an insufferable tool even then, but during junior year, he seemed to take things to a different level. Mick always had this smirk, like he couldn't wait to laugh at you behind your back, and I could tell he looked down on me and considered me a complete geek (which, to be fair, I was). He would regale us with tales of his possibly phony sexual conquests and at one point asked me about my girlfriend situation. "I've never had a girlfriend in high school," I replied. Big mistake.

Between Thanksgiving and Christmas 1995, I started receiving curious notes. The first note arrived while I was hanging out in the cafeteria during a pep rally, the place all the antisocial loser types went to avoid a crowd. Some guy walked by and dropped off a note, saying, "Hey, some girl wanted me to give you this." I opened the note and started reading.

Hello, I have seen you around school and I am really interested in you. Write me back. Sommer Malone.

I had never heard of Sommer Malone, so I went home and checked my yearbook. No one in there named Sommer Malone. I figured the whole thing was a prank, so I quickly forgot about it. A few days later, Hitchens gave me another of these letters in class, and since I had some basic trust in him, I responded. I asked some basic questions such as "Who are you? I couldn't find you in the yearbook. Why don't we meet up?"

There was always some internal logic in the replies: "My parents are strict and don't want me going on dates. We just moved here from Nashville so I'm new to Jefferson County Public Schools." Around Christmas, Sommer sent what seemed to be a final note saying she was moving back to Nashville, so I thought the whole thing was over.

I was wrong. Once January hit, the notes returned, with Sommer noting her parents had decided to stay in Louisville after all and we could resume talking. Around this time, Kane McGregor started getting in on the fun and started eating lunch with the rest of us. Kane was another senior and a buddy of Mick's. If I had to describe him, I would say he was Biff Tannen from *Back to the Future* come to life. A burly football player type, Kane relished tormenting me daily.

By this point, I figured at the least Mick, Kane, and Jim Hitchens were either pranking me or perhaps all of them knew this Sommer girl. I wasn't quite sure which. They knew too many details of the things I wrote about. I insisted to them I needed to meet Sommer, since otherwise this was a big waste of time.

Sure enough, they *did* produce Sommer, or at least someone posing as Sommer. Curiously, this girl even fit the basic description of the girl in the letters. Same basic height, reddish auburn hair, blue eyes. They introduced me to "Sommer" at a school function, and we said hello to each other and shook hands. That was such a bizarre experience. I still have no idea who she really was, but at the time, I felt relieved even though there was zero chemistry there whatsoever.

The notes continued for a while longer. They became more personal, more sexual in nature, and I responded in mutual fashion. Once a student office aide even delivered a note to me in the middle of U.S. History class. After a point, I started noticing other people in the lunchroom looking at me and entire tables full of people started laughing when I walked by. Obviously, not only was Sommer phony, but Mick and Kane clearly relished reading my notes to whatever seniors wanted to hear them.

Of all the seniors who heard about what was going on, only one stepped up to help me. That would be Melissa Bergman. I didn't know her at all, but she stopped me in the hallway after lunch one day. "You're Brian, right? What's your phone number? I have to talk to you about something important." I gave her my info.

Melissa called me that night. "Look, Brian. Sommer is not real. Mick made her up and Kane joined in as well. They've been reading all your notes to anyone who wants to listen in Mrs. Ballard's class. In fact, Mick almost got in trouble the other day when Mrs. Ballard asked about the notes he was reading to everyone."

"Yeah, I have been figuring out as much. God, why did I write all that stuff? This is so embarrassing."

"I finally had enough and figured I needed to tell you. From those notes, you seem like a really sweet guy. I even said to them he sounds like someone I would be interested in."

"Thanks for setting me straight on this, Melissa. I have some thinking to do."

If this had been a Hollywood movie, that conversation would be quite the nice "meet cute" scene. I would be kidding if I said this whole experience led to Melissa and me becoming an item, we lived happily ever after, but no. I maybe talked to her once or twice and then she drifted back to being someone I saw in the hallway and little more. I'll always be grateful to her for being the only one who tried to help me out. I had Mrs. Ballard for English senior year, and often wondered if she realized I was the topic of everyone's ridicule the previous year.

There was now destined to be a showdown with these guys at lunch the next day. I thought about jumping Mick Logsdon and beating him repeatedly with my lunch tray, but then thought better of that idea because Kane McGregor would start strangling me given his size advantage. Besides, why get suspended over these two creeps?

The epic showdown turned out to be nothing of the sort. There was no "Meet me in the parking lot at 3:00!" I told them Melissa had clued me in once and for all that there was no Sommer Malone, and this would be the final time I would eat lunch with the group. And to be sure, Mick and Kane laughed their asses off about this, before Mick asked, "Why did you believe any of this Sommer shit in the first place?"

"Maybe because I kinda wanted to?" Afterward, I started eating lunch with David Martini (a guy from German class) and some other people.

There was a surreal aspect to this entire fiasco. I quite enjoyed reading those notes from "Sommer." Several of them were quite well written, which made me wonder who was writing them. Were Mick and Kane the only writers, or did they have some female accomplice I never found out about? The more crude, sexual notes may have been Kane since those seemed more his style. But hey, if Mick Logsdon wrote those notes, I would say he could write a good love letter from the point of view of a fifteen-year-old girl. That's about the only compliment I will ever give him, however.

How nice it would be to say that was the end of this experience, but Mick and Kane kept bothering me. Mick offered a bizarre apology and asked if I wanted to go with them to a car show, but I told him no chance. The two of them found my morning hangout before the bell rang and made a point of taunting and tormenting me there as well, with Mick being the psychological bully who teased and verbally bothered me while smirking, and Kane being the physical bully who enjoyed getting in my space, grabbing my shirt, and shoving me against the wall. I never told any teachers or admins about this, mainly because I was already embarrassed by the notes. I didn't know how to explain the situation. I never felt 100% comfortable the rest of the school year, always on the lookout for those two and whatever antics they might pull. I felt relieved when the school year was nearly over and the seniors had left, so I never had to see either of them again.

Strangely enough, whether as a reaction to all of this angst or some other reason, that same time period coincided with my creative juices starting to flow. During that school year, I started writing a film script, which I titled *Welcome to Paradise* after the Green Day song. The script featured Jim Hitchens's wacky Reverend Emerson Biggins character he performed during lunch that year, at least before things went south and I quit sitting with the group.

I was also involved with a hilarious *Great Gatsby* video for Mrs.

Guthermuth's English class. For a group assignment on the last two chapters of the book, we decided to make a Quentin Tarantino–style violent version of the ending. Our group met up at Chris Owens's grandparents' house where we filmed this insanity. Our group fit the roles we had well: I played Gatsby, Owens was Nick Carraway, Jim Nord was Tom Buchanan, Katarina Crisp was Myrtle Wilson, and Angela Mayberry was Daisy Buchanan (she had little to do aside from hitting Katarina with the car in slow motion). I thought I would have been better as Nick Carraway and Owens as Gatsby, but since he was filming, I took the bigger role.

We took some liberties with Fitzgerald's text as Owens's Snoit bandmate Brian Corbin (a senior who wasn't even in the class) played George Wilson and cut me in half with a chainsaw (lots of ketchup blood!), and then blew Gatsby's brains out as someone threw fake brains at the camera. When we showed the video in class, it absolutely brought the house down. That was one of the highlights of junior year and I wish I had a copy, but Katarina couldn't find the tape in her garage when I asked about it some years ago. I guess our *Gatsby* video is now lost in time. This project, along with my writing, set in motion a dream of becoming a writer or director in the film industry.

I suppose the reason for mentioning these creative aspects is an attempt to find some kind of silver lining in a trying year of high school. Maybe I should have retaliated against Mick and Kane with some ingenious plan of my own? Or I should have hooked up with Melissa, or any other movie-style cliches? But that isn't how real life works sometimes. It baffled me as to why Jim Hitchens willingly played a part in this plan. (Jim Nord, for his part, didn't, or at least not beyond semi knowing about it). I more or less made amends with Hitchens, who said he was "trying to set me straight" even while acting as the go between delivering notes. We were still friendly during senior year, but his role in the entire Sommer Malone humiliation was a major reason I never kept in touch with him after high school. I ran into him once or twice at U of L, but otherwise I haven't spoken to him in years.

This might sound odd, but I have a strange nostalgia for that year of high school, even though it is in some ways harrowing to relive. Junior year was the first time I dedicated myself to taking school seriously, aside from refusing to read *The Dollmaker* in Mrs. G's class. She assigned the book as reading over spring break, and I had zero desire to read a 600-page novel over spring break. I had a script to write. Thankfully, I found the movie version with Jane Fonda and watched the VHS the night before the test and managed an 88% on it.

I also qualified for Governor's Scholars junior year and angered my counselor, Ms. Pennington, when I listened to the presentation and rejected it outright ("I have to spend five weeks in the summer up at NKU doing school related stuff? Nah, I'm good."). As fate would intervene, I wouldn't have been able to go to NKU for Governor's Scholars anyway. I also took a typing class that year, old-school style on a typewriter, and it was a life-changing class. There was life before I knew how to type, and life after.

But most of all, when I look back at junior year, it was a time when I was longing for Sommer Malone, a girl who at the end of the day wasn't attainable. Huh. Maybe I was more Gatsby than Nick Carraway, after all.

CHAPTER 3

THE YEARBOOK

January 2023. The other night I couldn't sleep, tossing and turning in bed, even getting up in a sweat thinking about half remembered foolishness which defined the end of my high school days. These ridiculous moments can stay with you over the years. The next day, I dusted off my senior yearbook from Butler Traditional High School, revisiting what people had to say about me. Before discussing the antics surrounding the yearbook, some backstory is necessary to explain my mental and emotional state during that time period.

Everything that happened in my life from roughly June 1, 1996 until June 1, 1997 can barely be done justice in writing, but suffice to say my dad suffered a paralyzing stroke with three days left in my junior year of high school.He had been stressed out for months over my grandmother Katie Lee's death and was remodeling her rickety house in Henderson, Kentucky, for reasons still baffling to me. My aunt Retta lived down the street and happened to walk by. She found him lying motionless on the living room floor, but quickly called for an ambulance.

Grandma's death in February 1996 coincided with the start of state KERA testing, so I went to the visitation in Union County and rushed back to Louisville. I did so because we were promised to beexempt from taking finals if we scored at least proficient on the KERA test. Of course, I ended up for whatever reason not being proficient, so I rushed back from Henderson after his stroke to take the finals I should have been exempt from taking in the first place. The school exempted me from taking the two I missed while out of town, but I still had to take the other four.

I certainly wasn't moving to Henderson for my senior year of high school, nor did it make sense to stay there given I was destined to go to U of L since my mom worked there and I would receive free tuition. I spent the summer going back and forth from Louisville to Evansville where my dad was at Deaconess Hospital. He was transferred to a Louisville nursing home/rehab center in late August. My mom, brother, and I went to see him for the first few months of school until he was released around Thanksgiving. During those first months of senior year, I passed my driver's test, albeit on the third try.

While my mom and I were in Henderson, my paternal grandfather, Grandpa Joe, also died in North Carolina. I found out when his second wife, Aunt Polly, called to tell us. I told her we were preoccupied with my dad's condition, so we couldn't attend the funeral.

"The doctor said his left side is paralyzed, but he's out of the woods at least," I said.

She understood, but her tone was full of a certain malice. "So you all can now push Danny around in a wheelchair and take him to stores?? Won't that be *nice*?" This conversation was the last time I ever spoke to Polly.

Making matters even worse, I became violently ill in December. I still don't know what happened other than eating bad tacos from Taco Bell one night. My dad's car salesman friend, Bob Crenna, came over to watch the UK/Purdue basketball game with Taco Bell on the menu. Crenna was my dad's first visitor after coming home. I felt slightly queasy later that night, and the next day I came down with the worst case of diarrhea during a test in Humanities. I rushed to turn in my paper to Mrs. Gutermuth and immediately ran to the bathroom. I asked to go home, soiled my pants rushing there, and then spent three days in and out of the bathroom.

I felt awful for a month, with stomach trouble on and off. I should have gone to the hospital, but never did. I was sick of hospitals by then. Even to this day, I still have a slight nagging pain in my right side, so I wonder if I tore a muscle. For years, whenever my dad wanted to eat at Taco Bell, he was always perplexed as to why I didn't want to go.

Fast forward to early March and the worst flood in Louisville since 1937. When it rains it pours, and we weren't spared that indignity either. Our apartment at Tanglewood off Fern Valley Road was flooded and we had to be evacuated by Army trucks to Atherton High School in the middle of the night, and then spent the next two weeks essentially homeless. The district didn't even cancel school on Monday, which I missed because I didn't have any school clothes to wear and because my Oldsmobile was partially underwater. The flooding itself wasn't the main disaster, but instead the idiots who insisted on replacing the carpet in the apartment. They ripped up everything and left all our belongings in shambles to the point where the apartment was uninhabitable.

We bounced around from a local Red Roof Inn to my maternal grandmother's house until we hired some movers to take all our stuff from the old apartment to the new one, which at least happened to be next door. I wanted to stay longer at my grandma's, but she kicked us out after a certain point. In fact, she did so right after U of L beat New Mexico 64–63 in the second round of the NCAA tournament.

"This is not your home," she said.

Being kicked out of my grandma's house was hitting rock bottom. I now understand how stressed she felt having us there for days on end, though. The house wasn't accessible for my dad until 2003. We made up with her by the time spring break rolled around, and I stayed over to watch the NCAA title game, where UK blew their chance at what would have been a threepeat by losing in overtime to Arizona. If Rick Pitino had only played Derek Anderson...

On a lesser note, my senior year of high school didn't have much of a soundtrack to it. For the first three years of high school, my favorite radio station was WQMF2 105.9, Louisville's modern rock station, which played everything from '90s alternative to '80s New Wave, even older punk rock. In September 1996, the station switched formats to Top 40 adult contemporary. I still miss QMF2 to this day. To me, it was the best radio station ever. But this development wasn't shocking. The '90s alt rock movement was fading by the time senior year rolled around. The first month of my freshman year? Nirvana's *In Utero,* my favorite album, was #1 on the charts. By senior year? "The Macarena" was the most popular song on the planet and the Spice Girls were riding high.

I suppose the point in mentioning these events is to give some background into my mental and emotional state circa 1996–97. I felt like I was going crazy, and to most people at Butler High School, they no doubt thought I *was* crazy. I spent my senior year of high school weirding out everyone I could find. I went around telling people in class "Smell my butt!" I even wrote a story about these antics in Creative Writing, only to have Mrs. Ederheimer refuse to accept it. I went around with a piece of folded paper I called a "magic square" which had the words cabbage, cheese, hair, and teeth written on it for no apparent reason. I wrote poems, some good, some bad. I wrote demented short stories. I wrote a film script based on classmate Chris Owens's story he wrote in Creative Writing (a *1984* knock off I titled *Project Ziola*).

I even gave my English teacher, Mrs. Ballard, a cabbage for Christmas. She laughed uproariously, then took it home and made coleslaw out of it. I became such a teacher's pet in English that Owens, in his inimitable fashion unleashed, "Yes, yes! Kill Mr. Ballard! Kill Mr. Ballard and take his place!"

"What?!" I said.

You'd be hard-pressed to find someone in any of my classes senior year who didn't think I was a lunatic, but not the sort of bad boy, punk rock lunatic like Owens, who had a cool factor. I was too square to fit in fully with that crowd, too straight edge. As one Creative Writing classmate said in my yearbook, "You're a really good writer when you aren't being perverted." Hey, that's me at my best!

Suffice to say, this sort of behavior wasn't exactly attractive to girls, or, I have no idea if it was or not since I had zero clue how to talk to girls beyond mundane matters. I did have my eye on a few, though. There were two in particular who stood out to me. One was Jessica Herbert, a tall, stunning brunette who looked like someone straight out of old Hollywood and spoke like Scarlett O'Hara, if you took out the bitchy attitude. The other was Tracy Bowen, a fun blonde girl with a bubbly smile and who was also the class president during our sophomore and junior years.

Jessica made sense on paper. Our moms were in the same graduating class at Valley in 1969. She lived about three minutes from my grandma's house in Prairie Village. During freshman year, she hung out at Beechmont and watched my baseball games, although I could speculate she and another girl went there to check out All Star catcher Eddie Happ more than me.

During sophomore year, we had several conversations about old movies and current music, and I thought we had some things in common. Jessica had a talent for dipping her toes in geeky stuff like 1930s movies without becoming ostracized as a nerd, whereas I jumped in headfirst with discussions of having Wheeler & Woolsey festivals. We didn't have as many classes together junior year, and by senior year we only had Mr. Unterreiner's Government & Economics class.

I knew Tracy from freshman year Health/PE class, but I don't think I so much as said hi to her sophomore or junior years. By senior year, she was in two classes with me—Humanities and Creative Writing. She sat next to me in Humanities, in a cluster where I was the lone guy with Tracy and four other girls. I had a blast in that class, engaging in all my antics and bewildering the girls. At a time in my life when everything seemed to be falling apart, I at least enjoyed being at school. Butler was a desperately needed structure, a refuge from the chaos going on in my home life.

To be blunt, both of these girls were entirely out of my league. But what's a league? I didn't even have a league. I hadn't even signed up to play or paid the registration fees. Not helping matters, I had a terrible case of cystic acne during senior year, made worse by secondhand nicotine withdraw after my dad's stroke, given he was a chain smoker. I started Accutane by the time I began college, but this was a constant and even painful problem senior year and a real blow to my self-esteem. I still felt the need to say something to one of them before senior year was finished. I liked Jessica throughout our four years of high school, but I always felt anxious or even intimidated around her, through no fault of her own. I wouldn't say the same thing about Tracy, but instead viewed her as a gal pal with whom I could act goofy.

By the time May rolled around, time was running out to tell Jessica or Tracy how I felt. I hatched out a plan with Jim Hitchens on the seniors' Belle of Louisville trip. Some schools planned a senior trip to Kings Island in Cincinnati, or at least to Kentucky Kingdom here in town. Butler seniors got to freeze on the deck of the Belle while trav- eling down the Ohio River, which even in the middle of May was chilly at night. After scoffing at Hanson's newly released single "MMMBop," I told him I planned on writing everything I felt down in Jessica's year- book at the upcoming Sunday signing party, where we were to pick up our caps and gowns.

"That wouldn't be my approach, but hey, man, you do you," Jim said.

I was conflicted but decided to go ahead with the plan.

Sunday, May 18, 1997. A day that will live in infamy in the annals of Butler High School. I went ahead with the plan, foolish as it may have been. I signed several yearbooks, had mine signed in return, then finally made my way to Jessica. I laid the schmaltz on thick: "Jessica, you are the single most stunning girl I have ever seen in my life. You are also one of the kindest, nicest girls I've ever met, the epitome of class, and I have had a crush on you ever since freshman year." This rambling went on and on, but I got it out of my system and, most importantly, left my phone number.

A funny thing happened, though. I exchanged yearbooks with

Tracy as well before I left and once it was in front of me, something similar spilled out. I hadn't planned on this, but once I started, I let the passion flow. Soon after signing Tracy's yearbook, I bolted. I figured things were about to get weird, so I decided to head home.

The next day was interesting to say the least. In Humanities class, I was already seated, and Tracy came in, sat down, and immediately smacked me right on the shoulder. "Hey! What's the meaning of all that stuff you wrote in my yearbook!?"

I didn't quite know what to say other than, "I guess it was how I felt at the time."

"How you feel about me, huh? You wrote the same thing in Jessica Herbert's yearbook!" Yeah, I was screwed. They had apparently compared notes. Thankfully, Mrs. G. saw what was going on and started class, a study hall for the upcoming final.

During class, I pulled out a piece of paper and a pencil and started writing. I exchanged notes back and forth with Tracy to the point where she understood where I was coming from. She was not some second option, not a consolation prize. I had a hard time verbalizing this sort of thing, but on paper I could spin doctor with the best of them. By the end of class, she gave me her phone number, we both smiled at each other, and I left thinking, "Wait, did that actually *work*?!" The class started out with me being beaten and yelled at, and ended up being one of the most magical classes I have ever been in. For the first time in months, it felt so good to be alive.

I still had Jessica to deal with, and even twenty-five-plus years later I can't quite figure out her reaction. Whereas Tracy acted in a way I thought someone might in such a situation, Jessica said nothing to me in Mr. U's Government & Economics class. I left class as vexed as I went in. I hadn't counted on her saying nothing at all. Even cussing me out would have been something, and I would have known for sure where I stood. Perhaps I should have realized the lack of a response *was* the response. But I wasn't too worried yet since I at least had something brewing with Tracy.

That night I tried calling Tracy to tell her Jessica had ghosted me and thus we were a go, but she wasn't home, and I talked to her mom (pre-cell phones, folks. The struggle was real). The next day in class I told her about the call, which she had missed being out with some friends. As class went on, I overheard Tracy and two other girls talking about some guy, no idea who, how hot they thought he was, how they wanted to know him better, and so on. I didn't care whether the other two had this conversation, but Tracy being involved while sitting next to me felt like a breach of.... something? While I wasn't on some moral high ground here, I thought I was trending in the right direction of being her boyfriend. As I sat there deflated, I figured there was nothing going on with Tracy. She didn't really care about me. What would a girl like her want with a misfit like me anyway? I whispered, "Tracy, the stuff I said, don't worry about it."

"Okay, I won't," she said. And that was that.

In the back of my mind, I still wondered about Jessica, though. I saw her in the hallway before school the day after Senior Awards Night.

"Hey, Brian. Congratulations on the awards you won last night." I had received an English medal as well as one for Mr. Orwick's German class.

"Thanks. What did you think of what I said in your yearbook?"

"Oh, it was nice of you. But I'm already talking to someone else."

"Hmm.... Well, can I have your phone number either way? We can keep in touch."

The bell toned to start heading to class. She walked away, but said, "Sure, but I can't write it right now. I'll give it to you later in class."

So, class went by and, once again, nothing. Didn't speak to me, no number, nothing. I was mighty confused. If she had zero interest, why not blow me off entirely instead of teasing me with the phone number? I still needed to know more. In retrospect, I realize I had put her in an awkward situation since she clearly wasn't interested, but I kept pressing the issue.

By this time, the school year was nearly over. Seniors took finals a week earlier than everyone else at Butler and the last four days after Memorial Day were a formality of activities and rehearsals. Our final senior function in the gym occurred the Tuesday after Memorial Day. A DJ played some tunes and we watched a bunch of clueless guys challenge the girls' volleyball team and get destroyed. This was my last chance.

I spotted Jessica in the bleachers sitting with Veronica Wilkerson, so I wandered up and sat behind them (Jessica and Veronica were coeditors of the yearbook). After working up some courage, I tapped Jessica on the shoulder and meekly asked, "Can I have your phone number now?" Her response was so chillingly cold I remember it vividly even today.

"What do you want it for?"

I was at a loss for words. I had never seen that side of her before. I mustered up, "Um, to call you, I guess."

"Look, I already told you I am talking to someone else."

She turned around and went back to watching the ongoing festivities, ignoring me completely. Soon after, I left the event, never feeling more humiliated. I won a CD at the event, some random collection of songs. I went home and listened to it on headphones. To this day, whenever I hear Pat Benatar's "Hit Me with Your Best Shot," I think back to that day and how Jessica Herbert certainly hit me with hers.

After that encounter, I wanted high school to be finished. Senior year had left me physically, mentally, and emotionally broken, with nothing more to give. At least WLRS, The Walrus, replaced QMF2 right after Memorial Day in 1997. After playing "I Am the Walrus" nonstop for a week, WLRS went on the air right before graduation. As I left Butler for the last time on Friday for graduation rehearsal at Freedom Hall, I turned on 102.3 and heard Veruca Salt's "Volcano Girls." This was a sign things were hopefully getting back to normal.

Graduation happened that overcast Saturday. My dad had a fever and didn't attend. I drove myself to Freedom Hall, with the rest of my family following later. Didn't get much of anything in terms of graduation gifts. I went there, received my diploma, and discussed the awful American dubbed version of *Mad Max* with people from homeroom. Chris Owens showed a rare moment of vulnerability for him. He was worried his ne'er-do-well mom, who left him with his grandparents so she could become a groupie for Ronnie James Dio era Black Sabbath, might yell out when his name was announced. I always remembered that. Even though graduation day was the last time I saw most of these people, I didn't say goodbye to anyone. I just left.

In the weeks following graduation, I went with my family to Myrtle Beach on our usual summer trip. After we returned, a long-delayed emotional collapse finally hit and I sank into darkness. I managed to fend it off back in January, when I missed several school days after mentally hitting the wall, but during the summer I crashed. After all that had happened, I was probably clinically depressed and in need of some help, but at the time none was forthcoming. The structure school provided was now gone.

I suppose I could have called Tracy anyway, but given my dark mood, what would I have even said? "Hey, wanna watch a movie? I have Sam Peckinpah's *Straw Dogs*. If that one is no good, I also have *Deliverance*. *Blue Velvet*? *A Clockwork Orange* perhaps?" I dunno. I figured pursuing Tracy would lead to nothing but heartbreak. What was I going to do? Invite her over to a disheveled apartment with our junk now scattered everywhere so she could see eye high mounds of VHS tapes? Or check out my dad's broken bedframe, with the mattress practically on the floor?

I felt as if I had failed high school. I didn't fail any classes, but I failed at nearly everything else. I failed to make the baseball team in my freshman year. I didn't go to any football or basketball games. Didn't go to either ring dance or prom. I met no lifelong friends who I would do anything for. Most of my classmates had either alienated me or I had alienated them. The phone wasn't going to ring. No one cared. Was that all high school had to offer? People put together in a building for four years to tear each other apart?

I didn't do anything to prepare for U of L. I didn't care. I didn't even want to get out of bed in the morning. In mid-August, someone from admissions called wanting to know if I was still coming, and if so, I needed to go to orientation. So I went to orientation and registered.

But I still didn't *care*, and only the 58% on my first test in Biology forced me to snap out of this dreary malaise, quit feeling sorry for myself, and get my act together. Over time, a new and better structure replaced the old one. College was tranquil compared to the madness of high school. I stopped acting like a lunatic, realizing the damage that had been done in terms of how others perceived me. I wanted to get lost in a crowd.

In retrospect, everything I did that last month of high school was ill-advised. Telling one girl in flowery prose you are madly in love with her is one thing, but the scenario is more awkward when you tell two girls this at the same time, at the same party, on the same day. Most of the heartache was self-inflicted to be sure. I could have said nothing of note, just wrote in both of their yearbooks "Nice knowing you for the past four years. Good luck in your future endeavors." Something with all the charm of a WWE talent release posted on a late Friday news dump. But somehow that isn't my style. There wasn't anywhere either scenario could have gone anyway. Jessica was destined to start WKU in the fall, Tracy off to Murray State. Would I have traveled two hours to Bowling Green or four hours to Murray to see either of them? People end up on different paths sometimes.

Having pulled out my old yearbook, I couldn't help but compare what Jessica and Tracy wrote. Jessica's entry was buried on one of the pages inside the binding and it was a typical "Nice to know you for four years, good luck" type thing. No hint of romantic feelings. Tracy, on the other hand, took up most of an entire page with large writing saying how I was in a class by myself, she wouldn't be surprised if I won major awards for writing (still waiting), and even finished with "Don't forget to smell my butt!" Sometimes we look at things with 20/20 hindsight, but one entry was written by a courteous friend and the other could have been, well, something more. Either way, you can't force someone to feel a certain way about you.

Jim Hitchens's yearbook entry was another highlight, written in the persona of his wacky pimp/preacher character Reverend Emerson

Biggins ("I am tired of living under The Man and The System. Only your stories will keep the Reverend alive, my brother.").

Chris Owens was his usual antisocial self, mainly spewing profanity before ending with "Fuck you, I hope the valedictorian dies!" There was also the previously mentioned "perverted" quote, and a whole lot of people commenting I was a nut, but also how I should "never change for anyone."

This was the legacy I left with most of these people. They never saw anything in me beyond that. They didn't see someone who helped out anyone struggling with a piece in Creative Writing, or someone glad to help out the crew in Humanities with whatever they were working on or being a player/coach in German class helping mentor other students. They saw a bizarre weirdo, which was primarily my doing. The way I acted during senior year was a baffling cry for help, but I don't think anyone knew how to listen.

To be fair, Owens wrote a rambling manifesto the last month of school, and he said something about me in it. "There are only a few people I have met at Butler I felt had any personal integrity and aren't sellouts. Brian Paige is one of them." Of course, he finished by also saying, "If I ever see any of you on the street in the years to come, I'm going to put my head down and walk on by like you don't exist." Owens now lives in L.A. and runs a music studio design company. I've tried various times to reach out to him over the years, but he rarely responds. I guess he was serious.

Over the years I have tried to reconnect with both Jessica and Tracy. Both are Facebook friends of mine, albeit one significantly more than the other. Jessica was a MySpace buddy before that since I reached out to her on there after her mom died in May 2007 and offered my condolences. I happened to see the obituary in the *Courier-Journal*, and I noticed it because I recognized her mom's picture from my mom's old 1969 Valley yearbook, which I saw about a decade earlier.

Both are married and have kids now. The last time I saw Tracy was at the ten-year reunion, and she was still fun to hang out with, although I felt awkward with her husband there, although he was a cool guy. At some point in the past ten years Tracy went full-blown into being a Christian conservative type, announcing her awakening in an epic Facebook post.

In 2015, shortly after the Obergefell Supreme Court ruling on gay marriage, Tracy posted a series of anti-gay links on Facebook, posts bashing gay marriage and so on. These posts became uncomfortable to the point where I sent her a private message asking her to please stop, she was coming off poorly. This was the first time I recall having a serious argument with her, but she stopped. At least she denounced Trump back in 2016. I'll give her that much. She doesn't post much on Facebook anymore, too busy raising four kids.

I tried reaching out to her for info when writing this piece. Her response?

"I'm sure it will be great, but I'm a married woman and I don't feel comfortable talking to men. I hope you understand."

Merely bringing up the topic triggered something, and she shut down. Some people change and there isn't anything you can do. Tracy feels lost to me now, even as a friend, and that is quite heartbreaking. The story of her struggles leading to her current worldview does interest me and I wish she had enough trust to tell me so I could understand.

As far as Jessica goes, she used to work at Jefferson Community and Technical College before moving to Indiana. She put in a good word for me when I applied for a job back in 2017, although I blew the interview. I sometimes share pieces of writing with her, and when she isn't too busy, she gives me her thoughts. Occasionally we still talk about old movies. While I wouldn't say we're close or exchange Christmas cards, I consider her a friend.

I often wondered what I would say to Jessica if I ran into her again, which eventually happened at the twenty-year reunion. After two decades, I bumped into her while going to get a beer, exchanged pleasantries about our kids, and then we talked about Boyz II Men's "I'll Make Love to You," which the DJ was playing at the time.

"At least they are playing songs appropriate to our years in high school," I said. "Back at the ten-year reunion, all they played was a bunch of '80s stuff and current songs." The same surface-level conversation we might have had throughout high school. Twenty years had gone by and that was all I had to say.

March 2023. Jessica posted something very real and serious on Facebook, openly discussing being the parent of a transgendered teen. "If you do not want to support my family or want to be political, feel free to unfriend me," she said.

The news wasn't shocking to anyone who has followed her posts, since the situation has been clear for a while. Her revelation was still overwhelming to read, and I sent her a message. I related my first memory of a trans student at Butler, Nordy, who was summarily kicked out of school during freshman year for being different. I also discussed a couple of trans students I knew from subbing at Manual, and how I called them whatever name they wanted to be called and did my best to treat them like individuals.

"So, do I support you and your family? Hell yes. Always."

Her response was phenomenal. "Most people in smallish-town Indiana are supportive, but there are a few close-minded assholes," she replied. She agreed Butler was an insidious place where she too never felt entirely at home. WKU was where she found "her people" and figured out what she stood for in life.

She discussed her thoughts on "The Season of Sommer," which I sent her weeks earlier. "I can't believe those kids did that to you, but kids can be cruel. If I was ever cruel to you back then, just know I'm so sorry. We all had our moments, and I had my fair share too. Thank you again for being so supportive and inclusive." This was the sort of next level, real-life discussion I always wanted to have with Jessica, or anyone else from high school. Jessica is someone of integrity and is a pretty great human being. I was right about her all along.

Senior year was a defining time in my life, for better or worse. I'm still the same misfit, the same frustrated writer, maybe even on a good day the same hopeless romantic. A little more mature perhaps, but not *too* much. The "good old days" weren't necessarily all that good, but they certainly mattered and made me who I am today. Earlier I bemoaned the notion that I didn't meet any lifelong friends in high school, but after all these years, I am still trying. Sometimes that effort produces more rejection. Sometimes it produces something special. But dammit, I am still trying. I guess some people never change. Not even if the floods come, and this is a lake.

CHAPTER 4

DIAMOND HORSESHOE

I graduated from the University of Louisville in 2001. The era was an inopportune time to graduate from college, given the economic prosperity of the 1990s was waning after the dot com bubble burst. This is a tale of a time when I was at a serious crossroads in life, but instead of picking a particular path, I decided to sit down on the side of the road. It is an era I do not look back on with much fondness or nostalgia, a time when I became fully immersed, for better or worse, in what the internet had to offer.

When discussing technology, I've always been playing catch-up. I spent most of my college years without any sort of home computer, relying on my old Smith-Corona typewriter to type most of my term papers, using the internet on campus at either the library or the computer lab in Strickler Hall. I didn't have home internet access until my junior year of college, and then I only had a WebTV I got for Christmas in 1999. I messed around with it for a year or so before getting a Compaq computer for Christmas in 2000. My parents understood nothing about computers. My dad never used them much when he was a car salesman, and my mom had left her job at U of L circa

1994 when she was approved for disability after being diagnosed with multiple sclerosis.

Once I obtained any sort of home internet access, I did what any twenty- or twenty-one-year-old guy would do: namely, I looked up wrestling dirt sheet news and started trading classic movies with fellow film buffs. Mind you, I didn't go in for copying factory tapes and posting them online. That sort of thing violated a moral code on some level. I went in for obscure 1930s and '40s titles, stuff not on video in any form. Films such as *Hellzapoppin, Love Me Tonight,* and *Trouble in Paradise* were shockingly popular. This was the internet of the early 2000s. It was the Wild West.

I met Arianne Walters in December 2000 when she inquired about a copy of the Betty Grable musical *Diamond Horseshoe*. What could have been any other trade became a whole lot more when Arianne started engaging me in email conversations. At first, I told her about myself. I was a college student at U of L, a big movie buff, into sports. I was excited to find someone my own age who shared this sort of interest. Most fellow film buffs were either middle-aged or senior citizens.

We kept emailing that holiday season, and even after I got the new computer, I kept the WebTV for the time being since the initial emails with her were on my email there. Arianne sent me a picture of herself, which I believe was a couple years old. She was about 5'7", had brown hair, and triple D sized breasts, which she later had reduced to a single D due to back pressure. In fact, her AOL email had DDD in it. Once I registered for AOL, I looked up her profile and it ended with a cryptic comment: "If you're into playing games, leave me alone." Given I already had geek buddies of mine petitioning me to play online games with them, I thought that's what she meant.

Before long, I was wild about Arianne. Not only was she a fellow film buff, but she was also politically similar in mindset, seemed focused on education, and also enjoyed a decent amount of the same music. Her favorite band was Letters to Cleo, which I found fascinating. She also liked Dave Matthews Band, which I found less fascinating. She also had taken Accutane for bad acne and understood the frustrations cystic acne could cause. She had a way of putting me at ease, of flirting without actually flirting.

I convinced her we should start talking on the phone. I didn't have a cell phone (and wouldn't until 2009, again playing tech catch-up), but I had a secondary phone line installed in my room. I bought some 10-10-220 cards at a nearby Chevron gas station for these long-distance conversations since Arianne lived in Northridge, California, part of Los Angeles's San Fernando Valley. Arianne was amused by my accent the first time we talked, which is odd since I never knew I had one.

Some of my classmates at U of L thought I was insane for being interested in a girl who lived so far away. One guy named Brad in my Persuasion class tried to persuade me against this idea: "There are plenty of girls as good as her, and guess what...they're here!" Fellow online wrestling buddy Mike Northern dismissed Arianne almost immediately after seeing her picture ("I dunno, man. She looks kind of skanky to me. Get your head on straight"). I even printed out AIM (AOL Instant Messenger) conversations and brought them to class for fellow students to do content analysis on whatever cryptic comments Arianne made I didn't quite grasp.

In my final undergrad semester at U of L, I took an absurd eighteen hours in order to graduate in May. Despite all these classes, I still agreed to also help Arianne out with her classes at a community college. Arianne was taking classes there with the idea of transferring to Cal State Northridge once she had enough credit hours. I didn't mind helping with her psychology class, but after a while, I was writing entire essays for her.

If she wanted a particular movie, I was glad to find it for her. She wanted to see the Jimmy Stewart/Ginger Rogers comedy *Vivacious Lady*, so I made a trade with someone and acquired a copy. She was desperate to see the 1966 Disney movie *The Ugly Dachshund*, since her own dog was similar to the one in the movie. That one was harder to find, so I bid an insane $60 for an out-of-print copy on eBay. Once the VHS arrived, it was a crappy LP mode tape, so I demanded a refund and sent it back. Yes, I made a copy first, violating my rule against such things. But, hey, in this case the seller misrepresented the item. Even my copy of a crap LP mode tape made for quite the birthday present (Arianne's birthday was February 2, Groundhog Day). She wrote, "I got your present in the mail today. I was grinning from ear to ear." Eventually, I found *The Ugly Dachshund* on TV and recorded a pristine SP mode copy off digital cable, then sent her the replacement tape. I demanded quality.

As the semester went on, I got to know Arianne better. In fact, I got to know her *too* well. This was a classic case of finding out entirely too much about someone and realizing I didn't have as much tolerance for certain things as I thought. During our various conversations, I found out some uncomfortable details:

1. Arianne lost her virginity at age thirteen to an eighteen-year-old guy. "I thought I was in love, LOL." This guy also visited her house and swore to her dad he had nothing but good intentions. After the fact, he blew her off and never saw her again. What astounded me the most was her dad didn't kick this guy out the minute he showed up. "Hey, I looked eighteen!"

2. At one point, Arianne dated a well-off thirty-five-year-old guy from the Hollywood Hills, but he had a difficult time getting an erection, so she cheated on him.

3. A couple of years earlier, Arianne had tried the long-distance thing with a guy from San Francisco and even went to visit him there. "We had an amazing physical and sexual relationship, but in person he was nothing like he was online. When I got back, I felt totally crushed, and thought I was pregnant, so I drank a lot."

4. She had smoked pot and done acid in the past but hated the acid. This didn't bother me *that* much compared to these other tidbits.

I had no idea what to make of these revelations. They went beyond any of my own experiences. When I was thirteen, I concerned myself with playing baseball and reading comics. In case all the discussion of film geekery had you fooled, I was still a virgin. I didn't know how to handle such information about someone I was interested in, maybe even in love with, so I acted like a complete dick. I called her up and proceeded to rant about all of these tidbits she revealed. "How dare you do this? I can't believe you did that! What is your problem?"

"So did you call me up to yell at me? Look, things are different out here than they are in Kentucky." I had watched *Fast Times at Ridge-mont High* that year and I couldn't help but think Jennifer Jason Leigh's character reminded me of Arianne, except Arianne was oddly cheerful when discussing these things. I think that was what set me off, her lack of pathos. I should have realized we were too different in mindset, but as Mike Northern noted, my head wasn't exactly on straight.

This sort of reaction also became quite the Catch-22. How could I convince Arianne I was different from these other guys when the eventual outcome involved one of us having to travel cross-country to see the other? Obviously, passionate lovemaking would be a desirable outcome, but where would things go after that? Would I unintentionally remind her of the uncaring guy from San Francisco? I was so confused. For someone who said she didn't like to play games, everything with Arianne was a game. A game I didn't know how to play, one I didn't understand.

I invited Arianne to my college graduation. She teased coming here for a few weeks, before saying, "There's no way my parents would let me travel all the way there for something like that." Instead, we decided I would come out to L.A. to see her shortly after graduation, right around Memorial Day. "I don't know how to feel about that. Flying from Louisville just to see me? Is there anything else you need to do out here?"

She posed an interesting question. I wanted to go to film school, but U of L didn't have a film program at the time. "I might also check out UCLA and see about their film and TV master's program. CSUN also has a post grad screenwriting program which sounds interesting, so

I might check it out since CSUN is where you are going at some point."

After double-checking with her to make sure the dates were okay, I went ahead and booked a flight to Burbank, since there was no way I flying into LAX. A couple of days after I made the reservation, Arianne wrote me an email with the following: "Hey, I hope you didn't already book the flight. My parents want to go on a camping trip Memorial Day weekend, and I won't be in town." I seethed over this. I asked her multiple times to double check the dates of the trip. Now I would have to pay $100 to switch the trip to some other time, and I had already paid for the plane tickets with my credit card. I thought about not even bothering to switch dates. I put the trip off for the time being since I was about to graduate, and after the school year ended, my parents wanted to go to Myrtle Beach.

Graduation itself was a bizarre day, back at Freedom Hall almost four years after being there for my high school graduation. A few of the same people were there who I knew in high school (Katarina Crisp, Veronica Wilkerson). We listened to the CEO of The Home Depot give an interminable thirty-minute-long speech, to the point where I was barely awake. My dad went to this graduation in his wheelchair, unlike the high school one when he was ill. He soiled his adult diaper during the graduation ceremony. I guess he wasn't thrilled with the Home Depot CEO, either.

My friend Chad Black was back in town from Florida that week, and he insisted on taking me, my friend Isaac, and some other guys on a strip joint odyssey to celebrate. I figured perhaps I was leading too sheltered of a life, so perhaps I should broaden my horizons. We made our way from the now defunct Trixie's, near where I lived on Preston Highway, to Déjà Vu on Taylor Boulevard, and finished the night slumming at the Thorobred Lounge on 7th Street. This was my first exposure to these establishments, and I was not comfortable talking to these women. Chad actively tried to pick up one stripper at Trixie's and would have ditched us, but decided not to since he was driving. Instead, we all got drunk and watched more of *New Jack City* on TV than the ladies dancing on the tables. We also drunkenly sang along to "Tuesday's Gone" and "Friends in Low Places" as we drove from one joint to another.

Chad also tried hitting on another stripper at Déjà Vu, but later revealed he backed off once she casually admitted to having chlamydia. I wasted $60 on three lap dances at Déjà Vu. I was hungry by the time we hit Thorobred Lounge and wanted food, but Chad advised against ordering anything. "Don't eat here. Not unless you want Harriet the Hand Job Queen cooking your food." I've never quite understood the appeal of strip joints. Talk about all build and no pay off, about like Paul Heyman's booking in ECW.

Anyway, with Arianne having frustrated me for the time being, I decided to try going out with some local girls I met online. I talked to one girl named Kelly, a Liberty High grad, who worked at Payless Shoes in Jefferson Mall, which went nowhere after she told me she was still having sex with her ex-boyfriend.

I met up with another girl named Jeanette and we saw *Tomb Raider* at the old Showcase Cinemas, discussed the works of Michael Jackson over dinner at Red Lobster, then went back to her place off Preston and Eastern Parkway. She and an older woman next door enticed me into smoking marijuana for the first (and, as of now, only) time, while listening to Cream's *Greatest Hits* and Black Sabbath's *Master of Reality*. This was 2001, not 1971. Much like strip clubs, I don't understand the appeal of weed. The joint gave me a headache, but it is nowhere near as intoxicating as an IPA. A few days later, I asked Jeanette if she wanted to do anything, and she said she would rather do her laundry than meet up with me again.

I talked to another girl named Sandy in July, and I still feel bad about how I treated her. We got along well initially and had some long phone conversations lasting until the morning. I went over to her house off Upper Hunters to watch Monday Night Raw, and as the show went on, we started making out on the couch in the basement. In between kisses, she asked me, "Do you think I'm pretty?" Uh...let me backtrack a moment. Sandy was a former 1996 Miss Louisville contestant, but by this point, she had put on considerable weight and had let herself go. When I had gone upstairs to go to the bathroom earlier that night, I noticed her Miss Louisville picture on the fridge. *Man, she was hot back then. What happened to her?* I thought to myself.

So, when asked this question, for some reason I couldn't tell her what she wanted to hear. My response? "Well, I think you were better looking five years ago."

"Aw, hell no!" she yelled, jumping up off the couch.

She went to the bedroom and fixed her hair back in a ponytail. Soon after, Raw ended and she said, "I think you need to leave now." So I did. When I arrived home, I found an email waiting from Sandy saying she never wanted to see me again. What the hell was wrong with me? Why was I engaging in self-sabotage? I told Arianne about this fiasco a few days later and she found it amusing. I told Chad as well and he ranted at me, "Dude, why didn't you just lie!? Get laid!"

My dad had a freak illness yet again that summer. I can't explain why this happened because I don't think even the doctors knew. He had been eating an insane amount of orange sherbet. My mom had noticed him dozing off at times, unable to stay awake or focused on anything. She took him to the hospital, where tests revealed his blood sugar had skyrocketed to the insanely high 1000 range that can cause a coma. Unlike my mom, he'd had zero history of diabetes before this episode. He was also having trouble swallowing liquids, with portions of whatever he drank going into his lungs. During his time at Audubon Hospital, gangrene set in on his paralyzed left leg and it had to be amputated. The doctor didn't even call us before cutting off his leg, instead calling after the fact to tell my mom: "Oh, we had to amputate your husband's leg." She was livid.

My dad spent the rest of the summer in either the dreadful nursing home Georgetown Manor or closer to home at Franciscan Rehab Center, which was considerably better. He had to eat mushy food and drink this thick and disgusting water in order to get his swallowing back under control.

Arianne was quite sympathetic and sweet during all of this turmoil.

To cheer me up, she even sent several "for your eyes only" pictures of herself. On some level, I still felt the need to go out to Los Angeles, to replan the trip. She was full of caution. "I'm not sure what I want. I'm afraid you'll do something to hurt me or I'll find a way to blow it." I talked with my dad in the hospital, and he felt getting away from this stress for a while was a good idea. There was nothing I could do about his ailments.

Thus, after months of delay, I planned the trip for August 21–28, right after my birthday on the 20th. My first plane trip ever, as well as the first time traveling to the West Coast. I was really going to do this. I was going to meet my Valley Girl, talk to these film people at UCLA and CSUN, and the future was unlimited.

CHAPTER 5

DIAMOND HORSESHOE: THE L.A. TRIP

Upon arriving at Standiford Field on Tuesday morning, I noticed how strangely lax I found the security at the airport. It was almost too casual, with family members being allowed to go all the way to the gate and not much in the way of security checkpoints. I had a layover in Dallas for an hour or so and was amazed at the size of the men's bathroom. There had to be fifty stalls in that restroom and all of the toilets were well cleaned and had lights to signal occupancy. Chef's kiss to the DFW airport. I needed help finding my gate, so I asked a security guard. She was a friendly seventy-something-year-old woman, and she pointed me in the right direction. I thought to myself, *If something crazy went down at this airport, what would she be able to do about it?*

The first thing I noticed upon landing in Burbank was the thick smog surrounding the entire city. I knew L.A. was smoggy, but this was jaw-dropping. Louisville is a polluted place with bad air as well, but this was on some other level. You could literally see pollution in the trees while on the freeway. My rental car was a compact Saturn, nothing amazing, but decent enough to drive around town. I quickly realized I couldn't drive on the L.A. freeways and stay sane. I have never seen anything like the sheer volume, or the speed, of traffic in Los Angeles. I managed to navigate I-5 to the 118 and arrived at my hotel off Sepulveda Boulevard. I stayed at the Mission Hills Inn, which is now known as the Valley Inn.

Once I settled in, I called Arianne to let her know I had arrived. I met up with her outside the hotel, an ominous sign of a future lack of intimacy. She had a Ford pickup truck, which I have to admit surprised me a little. Arianne was over two hundred pounds, but I already expected this since I knew about the car wreck a year or so earlier which had left her sedentary for a while. Almost immediately, things between us felt off. After some initial chitchat, we ventured to a nearby Chili's to eat. I scoured the menu, didn't see anything interesting, so I did what anyone would do when confronted with a lackluster menu: I ordered the cheeseburger. Upon doing so, Arianne slightly frowned and said, "A burger? *That's* what you're getting?"

We had a strange, awkward meal, and I began to understand what she meant by it being different to meet someone in person after talking online. Maybe there was too much pressure? We went to a Ralph's supermarket not far from my hotel so I could buy some food supplies for the week, and I couldn't help but notice how many open boxes were on the shelves. The Valley seemed like an area that was cooler about twenty years earlier but had since declined.

Once we got back to the hotel, we sat in the parking lot and talked for a while. "I brought a copy of *The Producers* since you talked about wanting to see the Broadway play."

"We'll have to watch it together at some point," she replied. Soon after, she casually threw out some bizarre news about things to come. "Hey, I'm going to be busy the next couple of days, so I will see you again Thursday or Friday." I already had a sinking feeling something wasn't right, that I had done something wrong. Despite my birthday being the prior day, Arianne didn't wish me a happy birthday or anything.

Since Arianne was "busy" for the next couple of days, I tried to think of anyone else I knew in the area. The only names I could recall were Tim and Linda Eleniak, a married couple who I sort of knew because Linda ran a Yahoo group dedicated to 1930s comedy team Wheeler & Woolsey. I had talked to Tim on the phone about three years earlier, and thankfully they were listed in the phone book. I gave them a call.

"Who is this?" Tim answered.

"This is Brian Paige. I don't know if you remember me, but we talked a few years ago about Wheeler & Woolsey. I'm here in town and wondered if you would like to meet up?"

"Sorry, but I had a heart attack about three years ago and I don't remember much from that time period. But hey, if you have something to contribute, feel free to stop by our house in Northridge tomorrow." Tim told me the address and I said I'd be there.

The next day I decided to check out UCLA's campus. I navigated the 405 to Westwood and was terrified most of the time. I decided I wasn't going to drive on the interstates again if I could possibly avoid doing so. I was going to die. I thought it was odd freeway on-ramps had traffic lights. I hadn't seen that sort of thing before. UCLA is in an elite area, not too far from Bel Air. No one was around in the film department when I went there, so I wandered around campus and checked my email at the campus library. On the way back to my hotel, I took the long way and went through Bel Air and Brentwood. After hearing about these areas for so many years, I found the reality unimpressive, to be honest. The houses may have been nice, but the land itself was ugly. I've been through the Lexington area and seen the lush, rolling hills of horse farms. Gated mansions with no breathing room in a desert didn't thrill me.

Whenever I traveled, I drove primarily on Sepulveda Boulevard, which runs parallel to the 405. Coming back from UCLA, I checked out most of the Valley. Sherman Oaks and Encino are the more affluent areas, with Sherman Oaks having the most amazing Target I've ever seen, complete with a parking garage. Panorama City and Pacoima are both crap and not worth going through. North Hollywood is bleh. Van Nuys is okay, although I wish I'd stopped by Sound City if I had only realized how close I was to it. The less said about the wasteland of Sun Valley the better.

Later that day, I ventured over to Tim and Linda's house. I had no particular agenda. I mostly wanted to see what sort of film memorabilia they had. Tim invited me in, and immediately said, "Hey, let's get something to eat. Then we'll come back here and I'll show you some stuff." We drove over to a nearby Carl's Jr., which to me is Hardee's.

Tim was a middle-aged man with graying hair and wore a striped green shirt with a pocket holding his glasses. He also wore a pair of gray shorts. He wore that same outfit whenever I saw him over the course of the week. Tim also had no problem talking about *any* subject with someone he had just met.

"Believe me, I know how it feels to be in a strange city. When Linda and I went to New York City a few years ago, there were creeps at every corner trying to sell kiddie porn to me. After a point, I begged them to stay away!"

"What did you do there?" I asked.

"Linda was modeling at a local club," Tim replied. "Linda usually does a stage act with retro 1920s jazz age vaudeville songs, but this turned into an impromptu modeling session since a photographer liked the way she looked in her leopard leotard. We were shocked to find out the club was a S & M place with weird fetish stuff going on everywhere, people receiving golden showers, other deranged things. Linda went ahead and performed, but the Hellfire Club was certainly a unique environment unlike anywhere else we've ever been."

Bear in mind, I was eating a burger and fries while he was regaling me with this story. I didn't know how to respond to any of this. I was too weirded out. I wondered to myself what kind of freaks are these people and what would happen if I went back to their house? Thankfully, nothing bad. I told them I went to the UCLA campus earlier in the day.

"That's great!" Linda exclaimed. "I went to UCLA. We recently saw a revival showing of *Follow Thru* there, which they have in a pristine two-color Technicolor print. Alas, we couldn't figure out a way to copy UCLA's master print."

"Yeah, but then UCLA got into some hot water soon after when they discussed showing *Birth of a Nation*," Tim replied. "That's the funny thing about any revival movie house around here. They always open up and talk about showing *Birth of a Nation*, then Jesse Jackson and the NAACP threaten a boycott and the theater backs down. They aren't even serious about showing the film. They tease showing it to get the theater's name out there, then show something less controversial."

Linda was several years younger than Tim, a rail-thin woman with reddish brown hair. Once we got back, Linda made me some herbal tea and they started showing me all sorts of old movie memorabilia. We definitely talked about Wheeler & Woolsey movies, and Tim blew my mind by showing me a clip from *Rio Rita* I hadn't seen before, a Bert Wheeler/Dorothy Lee music number called "Are You There?" It had been cut out of most existing prints. I was puzzled at Tim's apparent dislike of Dorothy Lee, as Tim revealed with some glee, "Woolsey told David Selznick that Dottie had no talent, so Selznick cut all of her numbers out of *Girl Crazy*." We finished the evening by watching a movie, but not a W & W movie. Instead, we viewed the Joe E. Brown comedy *Top Speed*. I also vowed to check out Eddie Brandt's Saturday Matinee while I was in town.

The following day I went to talk to one of the professors at CSUN about their screenwriting program. I emailed Kurt Starling to make an appointment, so he was expecting me. I met with him in his office at the Radio/Film/TV department on campus. I brought with me what I felt was my best work, my film script *Welcome to Paradise*.

"Hey, I'm glad to be here. I brought my script with me and figured I would leave it with you."

He gladly accepted it.

"I will have a look and be in touch with you in a week or so. But believe me, if you want to be involved in this industry, you have to move here. I have a hard enough time getting anything read and I'm in the belly of the beast. It's not easy."

There wasn't a huge amount to the meeting. He told me more about CSUN's program and I took a brochure. Whatever interest I had in the program depended on what he thought of the script itself. After the meeting, I gave myself a brief tour of the campus. CSUN wasn't quite on the same level as UCLA. However, CSUN seemed a more feasible option than UCLA.

I met up with Arianne again that evening for dinner and a movie. For some bizarre reason, she brought her cousin with her—a tall blond guy whose name escapes me, but he mentioned being in town until he had to go back to start school at UC Davis. The three of us had dinner at El Torito's Mexican Restaurant, where for the first time I experienced shredded beef in a burrito instead of ground beef.

Ironically, I struck up a conversation over dinner with Arianne's cousin about his ideas for online retail and other matters, whereas Arianne remained this mystery I couldn't figure out. Some things Arianne said to her cousin were eyebrow-raising, though. She implied one time some years earlier her parents had walked in on the two of them making out. Was everyone in Los Angeles some kind of freak?

For the record, we saw *American Pie 2*, the #1 movie at the box office at the time. After the movie was over, I followed them back to Arianne's house and the two of them went in the house, but she didn't invite me in. In fact, I was never invited into Arianne's house that entire week. At one point, I even mentioned this to Arianne, and she once again played the parents' card.

"My parents aren't comfortable with you being here."

"But they are okay with your sister having a live-in boyfriend?"

I don't think she ever grasped how hurt and offended I was over her failure to vouch for me.

That Friday, I kept my word to Tim and Linda and checked out Eddie Brandt's Saturday Matinee in North Hollywood. I didn't buy anything since I thought you had to be a member, but was fascinated, nonetheless. Here was a well-known store, listed in Leonard Maltin's book, celebrities frequented it for hard-to-find movies, and it was this hole-in-the-wall that sold bootlegs. This was classic film geekery at another level. Eddie Brandt's put my collection to shame.

Arianne picked me up later that evening so we could go to Hollywood. We checked out the Walk of Fame, Grauman's Chinese Theater, the works. By this point, I felt like I was imposing myself on her, but hoped to find some sort of spark we had in our emails and phone conversations. As we parked in a paid lot in Hollywood, the attendant asked if we were tourists from out of town.

"I am," I said.

"No, I'm an L.A. resident," Arianne replied.

"Oh, so you're his tour guide then?" the attendant asked.

"Pretty much," she replied.

This is starting to sound like a broken record, but Hollywood itself wasn't my cup of tea, not as a tourist, not as a would-be screenwriter or filmmaker, not as anything. The atmosphere was hectic with a ton of construction, and aesthetically, the iconic Hollywood Bowl or the Hollywood sign itself looked run down. I bought my mom and brother each a Hollywood-themed refrigerator magnet with their names on them, both of which still reside on the fridge at my mom's house to this day.

We ate at yet another burger joint, Shake Shack, which was more gourmet than the others. Back then, $20 was expensive for some burgers and fries, which I mentioned. This served to dig the hole even deeper with Arianne, who no doubt thought I was a cheapskate. Did it really matter? By now I had the feeling she placated me out of some sense of obligation. Once she dropped me off back at the hotel, we didn't make any plans for the weekend.

Since nothing was going on that Saturday, I called Tim and Linda and met them at a karaoke restaurant. Tim and I ate tortilla chips while Linda occasionally sang karaoke to whatever old 1920s jazz songs she brought. We made plans to make a day of it on Sunday, going to some celebrity gravesites as well as Chinatown.

Tim and Linda picked me up at the hotel in their car, which looked to be a rusty and barely functional 1983 Chevette. The first place we visited was Eden Memorial Park, right there in Mission Hills near my hotel. I was shocked to learn Groucho Marx's burial site was nearby. Groucho was one of numerous people whose ashes were interred at a mausoleum, which I found fascinating.

The bigger pilgrimage for us was Robert Woolsey's grave at Forest Lawn Cemetery in Glendale. Forest Lawn is quite the epic cemetery, a place where several celebrities of Hollywood past are buried (John Gilbert, Marie Dressler). The trip took a while in Tim's creaky Chevette, which terrified me on L.A. freeways since the car shook whenever it reached fifty miles per hour. I told them I once had this same problem with my car and the tires needed to be replaced. Once we arrived at Forest Lawn, I even agreed to buy some flowers to put on Woolsey's grave. This was one aspect of the trip that didn't disappoint. Forest Lawn is a beautiful, serene place.

Chinatown...not so much. Many places you see in movies and on TV are lackluster when you visit them. I bought some souvenirs at a store, such as an authentic bar of Chinese soap, as well as a massage roller. The $1500 samurai sword in the window display was too steep in price, however. What I remember about Chinatown most is the putrid smell of the place. The entire area smelled like a dumpster. We ate at Hop Louie's, which I had seen in the films *Lethal Weapon 4* and *Rush Hour*. The place was fine, I suppose, but no better than where I usually went for Chinese food back home—the now-defunct Golden Wall. "If you want really good Chinese food, you need to go to San Francisco," Tim said. "We went there when we got married years back and it was great."

When we returned to their house, I noticed some sketchy-looking guys near the end of the block. "Who are those guys?" I asked. "What are they doing here?"

"Probably drug dealers," Tim said in a matter-of-fact way. "We've had trouble with these guys dealing in the neighborhood."

Linda noticed my alarmed look. "This isn't Kentucky, Brian. Drugs are everywhere out here." Drugs are prevalent in Kentucky, too.

"I'm amused at how naïve you are, Brian. Going around L.A. with money in your pocket and not a care in the world. Typical dumb Southerner," Tim laughed. "Reminds me of when we went to New Orleans and how a friend of mine who lived there had a wad of cash out in public in the French Quarter and no one bothered him. I admired him in a way."

When we went back inside, something happened I will never, ever forget. Tim decided to show me his baseball card collection. "Wait here, I'll be back in minute," he said. When he came back, he handed me a 1952 Mickey Mantle Topps rookie card, protected in a glass case. There have been times in my life when I've been so shocked my jaw practically hit the floor, and this was one of them. I had seen this iconic card countless times since I as a kid, but never dreamed I would ever hold one in my hand. It was in near mint condition, too.

"I've been collecting the 1952 Topps set for years," he said. "I've got most of the major names too, all except Mays. I can't find Mays."

"You could always try eBay," I said. "They have everything on there."

I had one more full day left in Los Angeles. Tim and Linda invited me to come with them to Santa Monica the next day, once again in the rickety Chevette. At least we waited until after morning rush hour to head out, so for once the freeway was feasible to drive on. I thought about bringing my swim trunks, but Linda advised against that since she saw a polluted water advisory on the news that morning.

I found Santa Monica dystopian, to be honest. The overall atmosphere was ultra gentrified, with boutique shops and businesses all over the promenade, but with homeless people everywhere. These weren't the passive homeless people on the streets of Louisville, either. These were aggressive homeless people. As we left the car and walked near the pier, a dirty woman practically accosted me on the sidewalk begging for change. Startled, I gave her some. Perhaps I made a mistake wearing a polo shirt, dress slacks, and dress shoes. I looked like an out-of-town mark. We went to several shops and watched some of the street performers juggling or performing songs.

We also went on the pier itself, not riding any of the rides or anything but walking along until we got to the very end. As I stared out into the Pacific Ocean on that hazy day, I started realizing what an overall failure this trip had been. I appreciated Tim and Linda for taking me to all these places, but hanging out with a middle-aged couple wasn't quite what I had in mind when I planned the trip. Perhaps if the goal had been to meet up with fellow film geeks and go sightseeing, I might feel differently.

Tim and I discussed basketball at an outdoor eatery where we had lunch. Tim mentioned his uncle, Chuck Clusttka, had played for one of John Wooden's early UCLA teams. "One time I met Coach Wooden and asked him why he said nasty things about my uncle in his book. He asked, 'Who is your uncle?' to which I replied 'Chuck Clusttka.' 'Ah, that bum!' Wooden replied. It was hilarious." Of course, the conversation turned to the recently retired U of L coach, Denny Crum, and how he left UCLA for Louisville in 1971.

"There are still people in this town who hate Denny Crum for leaving for Louisville back then. We thought he would be the heir apparent to Wooden," Tim mentioned.

Once we arrived back at the hotel, I thanked Tim and Linda for their hospitality, shook Tim's hand, and gave Linda a hug goodbye. Tim told me if I ever came back to come stay with them. He would prefer having me around to Linda's mom, who spoke nothing but Spanish. "Linda's family aren't Mexicans or Puerto Ricans. They grew up in an area of New York City where no one speaks English." With that, I bid them adieu. I never took Tim up on his offer, perhaps due to some of the bizarre things he talked about, or the "dumb Southerner" remarks. I still talk to Linda on Facebook from time to time.

Later that night, I decided to call Arianne. She agreed to have breakfast with me at a local IHOP before I left for Burbank Airport. As I glanced at the menu, Arianne said, "You sure do worry about food prices." We had one final meal together. I don't remember much of what we said. It wasn't important anyway. After we drove back to her house, I took a picture of her for posterity. She thanked me for coming out to see her, gave me a hug, and that was the last time I ever saw Arianne Walters.

As the plane took off from Burbank, I noticed the huge cloud of smog as the plane lifted. I couldn't wait for the plane to fly higher in the sky where the air was cleaner. The trip back proved uneventful aside from the lasagna dinner on the plane. I needed uneventful. I had some thinking to do.

I had never felt so glad to be home. My mom picked me up at the airport and I spent the next few days unwinding from the trip, washing my clothes, and visiting my dad at Franciscan. He came home on Tuesday, September 11th, for a scheduled home nurse visit to review his new dietary restrictions. This was a precursor to him coming home full time. As the nurse talked to my dad, I watched SportsCenter in the living room. An anchor broke into the taped program with a live update, something about ongoing terrorist attacks. I immediately turned over to CBS and saw what was happening at the World Trade Center. We watched as the towers fell, the nurse reacting with more horror than my dad or me. We were stunned. The images didn't seem quite real. I've often wondered why my dad came home on that day of all days. The day seemed preordained. Later, my dad had to go back to Franciscan. I bought some gas at Chevron after he left.

I have a hard time remembering the next few weeks, since the entire country was in a daze. I instant messaged Arianne for a while after the trip, I suppose attempting to comfort her after 9/11. She was more or less curt with me by now, talking for a while before saying she needed to go, or had a date, whatever. I asked why she never said anything about my birthday, only to hear back, "Well, I bought a present for you, but it was delayed in the shop, and I never got it in time to give it to you." I told her not to bother.

Eventually, she came out and said, "Couldn't you tell I wasn't interested?" I sent an email back asking why, wondering where things had gone wrong. She replied with the one thing she knew would hurt me, knowing full well I had taken Accutane for cystic acne a four years earlier.

"I didn't like the scarring on your face and neck. You need to do something about that. It's a real turn off."

I'd finally had enough. I wrote one last email, accusing her of leading me on for months. There was no happiness to be found with her. She was the dark side of the force. I told her she didn't have to reply. She didn't. I've never talked to her again. I cancelled WebTV soon after, tossing the unit in the dumpster.

A week or so later, I heard from Kurt Starling at CSUN. He had read my script and was not impressed with it, feeling the main characters were unsympathetic pricks without much redeeming value. Well, you write what you know. I thanked him for his honesty, but any idea of applying to CSUN went out the window at that point.

I had no idea what direction to go in next. I had never felt so defeated. Whatever dreams I had built up in my head had come crashing down in spectacular fashion. I went out to L.A. to get the girl and to find a direction in life. I didn't get the girl, realized I didn't even want the girl, and didn't want to go back to Los Angeles ever again. This is a problem when trying to break into the film industry. I needed a new dream, but I never quite figured out what that might be. Instead, I kept going down the road to nowhere, scouring the internet for more females of dubious quality, and watched as this country descended into a post-9/11 bout of lunacy from which it has never fully recovered.

There have been times over the years, maybe late at night, when I become curious and do an internet search for Arianne. I don't know why since I don't want to reconnect with her. She is now married; I know that much. She also teaches as a part-time adjunct professor, which I have to admit mortifies me given back in 2001 I wrote several papers for her classes. Some of her online student reviews are amusing, though, with even the students recommending her taking note of her intimidating manner, bluntness, and sarcasm. I can certainly relate.

I tried not to let my experience with Arianne on that trip to Los Angeles break me, but all these years later I wonder if it did on some subconscious level. I even wonder, having recounted the sort of human being I had become circa 2001, if I was deserving of that rejection. I wasn't proud of myself. I still had a lot of growing up to do.

Despite Arianne's opinion to the contrary, I probably looked better in 2001 than I did five years earlier, but I couldn't say I was a better person. For most of high school and college, I thought I was a pretty good person, but after college I lost my way. I couldn't say that anymore. My high school and college sense of idealism gave way to a post-college, post-9/11 feeling of bitter cynicism lasting several years. Maybe that feeling never entirely went away. The world was changing in ways I didn't care for and that led to a feeling of being powerless. Some of my cynicism was also due to sending Arianne a copy of *Diamond Horseshoe*.

CHAPTER 6

THE SUB PAR FILMMAKER

To watch the movie clips discussed in this chapter, check out youtube.com/@Cabbageboy316 and http://y2u.be/l8r1-ypH3e0.

As 2005 ended, I needed to scratch my persistent itch and leap into the world of filmmaking. I had spent the better part of the preceding three years either selling movies on eBay or on my own now defunct website, Cabbageboy Movies. There was a finite audience for the sort of old classic stuff I sold, and even though 2005 was my most profitable year thanks to converting all my tapes to DVDs, this wasn't what I wanted to do with my life.

At long last I decided to apply to film schools. After talking to some of my professors at U of L, they wrote the necessary recommendations, and I took the GRE. I had three main schools in mind: UCLA, NYU, and Florida State. I visited UCLA in 2001, one of the preeminent film schools in the country. NYU was as well, with the Tisch School being a well-regarded program. FSU had a screenwriting tract that interested me, but I will admit it was my third choice.

Applying to graduate programs is a serious investment in time just to hear from these people. I submitted my applications, recommendations, and portfolios months ahead of time, then spent months wondering about my status. In the meantime, I also applied for the Directors Guild of America's Assistant Director program. For reasons I can't quite recall, I flew to Chicago to take a DGA test at the University of Illinois-Chicago.

I stayed at a Holiday Inn not too far from the Sears Tower, right in the heart of downtown Chicago, not far from the UIC campus. Feeling bored, I grabbed a cab and headed to the United Center for a Bulls/Rockets game. I spent the evening in the upper deck surrounded by French tourists thrilled at the idea of seeing an NBA game. They were more excited at the prospect of a free Big Mac if the Bulls won the game and scored 100 points. We cheered like crazy for the game to go into OT, where both teams surpassed the magic 100-point mark. Alas, the Rockets won 109-108 so no one got the free McDonald's food.

I made a mistake even going to this game. Chicago weather in January can turn brutally cold and snowy. I was warned by the cab driver not to head west of the United Center, so I hopped on a shuttle that took me back toward my hotel. Of course, I got off at the wrong stop and wound up slogging through the eerily deserted streets of downtown Chicago at 11 p.m., at least until I found another cab back to the hotel. I spent the evening freezing cold, shivering under the covers, trying to warm up.

Chicago is perhaps the single scariest city I have ever been to, and I've seen some bad areas of St. Louis and Baltimore. I was alone in Chicago, and in freezing cold January, the city has an ominous feel. The test itself proved uneventful, but I made the mistake of walking back to the hotel rather than hailing a cab. I passed a bus depot and found myself surrounded by a group of shady-looking black men.

"Hey, man. Do you have some money you can spare? I need to catch this bus out of town. Twenty bucks would be good." I assessed the situation and saw the rest of these guys staring a hole in me.

"Uh, sure. Here you go," I said, with some trepidation. I gave this guy twenty bucks out of my wallet. I walked briskly away and crossed the street. None of them followed me, but that day was the closest I have ever felt to being held up. To be fair, there were no weapons or direct threats involved. I was rattled, and still freezing cold, but after eating some pizza at the hotel, I navigated through some homeless guys living under an overpass and checked out the view at the top of the Sears Tower.

Chicago was an interesting experience. I've never been back, although I would return if I could stay around Wrigley Field and go to a Cubs game. As far as the DGA program goes, it ended up being a whole lot of nothing. About a month later, I received a rejection letter in the mail, which I quickly forgot about since I was more preoccupied with UCLA, NYU, and FSU.

I heard from the schools in early March. In what may not be a shock, I was routinely rejected by both UCLA and NYU. I still had FSU, though, and sure enough I received a letter inviting me to come down to Tallahassee for a formal interview along with several other candidates. With little notice, I paid for a plane ticket and hotel and made my plans.

I didn't know how to prepare for the interview since it was the first film school interview I had ever been granted. I watched Syracuse's improbable Big East tournament run on the hotel TV and went to a local book and music store where I bought Mudhoney's latest album *Under a Billion Suns*. I also drove around the FSU campus and tried to find the film program, which was located inside Doak Campbell Stadium. Somehow I wasn't surprised FSU would house their film school inside the football stadium.

Thankfully, the interview was on a Saturday in March, so there weren't many people around. I managed to find the entrance easily enough since I could see people filming on sets created underneath the bleachers. The offices themselves were as much a part of Doak Campbell Stadium as the football program. The office featured posters of various student films along with theatrical releases FSU alums produced (*Finding Forrester, Little Black Book*).

There wasn't a ton to the process, only a brief talk with some of the higher-ups in the department. They asked some curious questions: "What is an overrated film you have seen in recent years?"

"*Million Dollar Baby*. I thought it sucked. No one can attack an opponent in a boxing match after the bell, cause permanent damage, and face no repercussions."

"Who is a director you find overrated?"

"Nicholas Ray. I find his stuff too mannered and boring. Would anyone seriously rank *They Live by Night* over *Gun Crazy*? I don't even like *Rebel Without a Cause* much." These questions puzzled me. Why spend so much time asking about films and directors I didn't enjoy?

The main task involved being put in a group with the other applicants and quickly brainstorming a film plot. The people around me discussed a routine romantic comedy about a couple's marriage. When my time to chime in came, I said we needed some tension at the wedding ceremony and suggested adding Sergio Leone–style close-ups and Ennio Morricone music. I thought those were amusing additions, but I have no idea how well my ideas went over. Soon after, the interview was complete. Now the waiting game began to see whether I had sufficiently thrilled the committee.

A few weeks later, I received an answer. I had not. The letter was more ambiguous than a typical rejection. I wasn't one of the initial picks but was listed as an alternate. I have no idea if they told everyone something similar, but there remained some sliver of hope someone might back out or be unable to attend. Still, the frustration was growing inside me. Over time, I heard nothing else from FSU, so I gave up on the idea of being an alternate. I badly wanted to go to film school, if for no other reason than to escape Louisville.

I had dealt with my dad being in a wheelchair for a solid decade, as well as my mom's slowly declining health due to a combination of multiple sclerosis and diabetes. At least I had my own apartment, since my parents and brother moved into my grandma's house in Prairie Village after her death in 2003. I stayed at Tanglewood Apartments, moving to a one-bedroom unit in a different building. It was on the second floor, so there was no risk of flooding.

I could do my website related matters during the day, but my brother, Eric, was a truant by the time he went to Valley High School.

As such, I never entirely got used to living alone, but instead spent most nights at my mom's house to ensure Eric went to school the next morning since she couldn't force him. My mom had this curious faith in Jefferson County Public Schools, perhaps viewing it through the rose-colored lens of her experiences there in the 1960s. I never could explain to her Valley was now a dreadful school, nothing like what she remembered.

After three crappy middle schools in three years (Thomas Jefferson, Southern Middle, and Stuart), Eric's mind was mush. As for me, I felt increasingly frustrated and angry, my patience running thin. I felt as though I had outgrown Louisville. I needed to get away.

With no news on the FSU front, I took matters into my own hands and launched a film project based on my decade-old script, *Welcome to Paradise*. The project interested a friend of mine, Isaac Long. He went with me to Murphy's Camera on Bardstown Road to buy a Canon XL2 to shoot this magnum opus. Four thousand dollars was an awful lot of money for a camera, but I felt it was a decent investment. The Canon XL2 was the top prosumer camera on the market, which meant it was too expensive for typical home movies, but not good enough for serious filmmaking. It had two key features for my purposes: a 16:9 ratio to give a widescreen look and 24 frames per second, which gave footage a cinematic feel. The salesman at Murphy's seemed thrilled to sell one, saying, "You boys are on your way."

I played around with the Canon XL2, trying to figure out the settings. For all the hype of 16:9 and 24 fps, the camera had some serious drawbacks. Only auto mode produced acceptable lighting. The overexposure was terrible, and the darkened indoor setting looked too grainy. Worst of all, the camera's internal mic was useless. I quickly gave up and ordered a condenser mic. Even after that, serious editing work was required to raise the volume to something tolerable.

I convinced my friend Chad Black to read for one of the leads, Chris (a character based on Chris Owens, the edgy local rocker I knew in high school). Chad had become increasingly erratic and unreliable during what he now refers to as his "drug years" of the mid-2000s. I recall going to see *Sin City* with him at Stonybrook the previous year. He passed out midway through the movie only to wake up and wonder what Bruce Willis and Jessica Alba were doing. During the same period, I recall going to his apartment near Stonybrook, which he shared with a group of other people, and was stunned to hear talk of "doing lines." What I thought was a saltshaker on the living room table turned out to be something else entirely.

The idea was to have Isaac portray the drug addict character Brad, with Chad as Brad's best friend, Chris. I made things up as I went along. I filmed Chad in a car scene going through some lines. He wasn't great and wasn't physically right for the role either. Chad was a dead ringer for Farva in *Super Troopers*. That summer, Chad and Isaac agreed to film a key scene where both main characters are tied up in a basement. We were going to film the scene at Isaac's house, not far from U of L.

Sure enough, Sunday arrived, and Chad didn't answer the phone. Hours passed while I became increasingly frustrated and worried, until it became obvious we weren't going to film that day. I gave him one last call and he finally answered.

"Hey, man. Sorry, I fell asleep and missed your other calls. I can't really do this today. We'll film some other time."

On the surface, this wasn't a big deal, but given the stress I had put on myself, I flat-out had a breakdown after hanging up the phone. The various school rejections, the constant stress of my family situation, all of it was too much. I sat down at my mom's dining room table and started bawling, almost hyperventilating from being so upset. My mom was utterly baffled.

"What in the world is wrong with you?"

"I feel like such a total failure. *Nothing* works out the way I have it in my head. No one cares about this stuff the way I do."

"You aren't a failure. Stop talking like that," she said, almost breaking down herself.

"What else would you call me? I'm almost twenty-seven. I can't seem to get into any film schools. I sell bootleg movies on eBay to make

SALVAGED FROM THE FLOOD

ends meet." I went into the bedroom and laid down. After a while, I came back to reality, realizing Chad wasn't reliable enough for such a major role. I never gave up on the idea of him being in the film, but in a supporting hitman role or maybe as the hulking bodyguard, Gustav.

I needed some other people who had experience making videos here in town. To that end, I managed to find some contact info for an old high school acquaintance, Jimmy Humphrey, on MySpace. I knew Jimmy from German class in high school, and I kept tabs on him from afar while in college. Jimmy used to write a comic strip for *The Cardinal* student newspaper, amusingly entitled *I Eat Poop*. I remember my newswriting professor Vince Staten ranting, "How does an otherwise reputable publication like *The Cardinal* allow that kind of trash to be printed in it?" *I Eat Poop* became a local access TV show with various wacky antics and spoofs with Jimmy and his friends. I gave him a call to gauge his interest.

"Hey, Jimmy. This is Brian Paige. I'm planning to shoot my own movie and I need actors. Would you be interested?"

"Maybe. I'm also doing my own project but send me the script and I'll have a look."

"Okay, cool. Right now, I need someone to play the role of Chris for a key scene. You don't have much dialogue to memorize."

I sent Jimmy the script and told him to take note of the basement scene with Brad and Chris, which we would film first. A few days later, Jimmy wrote back saying he was ready to go. In the meantime, I went shopping at a local Ace Hardware for supplies: lighting equipment, a rope to tie up Isaac and Jimmy, and a box where the main character hid his stash of drugs. Now I had the props, the cast, and the camera. We were ready, or at least so I thought.

By mid-June we were ready to film. Isaac had acted in community theater in Elizabethtown, so I figured he had some idea what he was doing. Eric was drafted to be the sound man. We arrived at Isaac's house to film the basement scene to find out Isaac hadn't memorized any lines. He hadn't even read the script. This was not good, since ninety percent of the scene was Brad's monologue about witnessing a terrifying rape and murder while in a drug-induced stupor. It was the critical scene of the entire script.

Isaac had major issues going on in his private life. He and his wife, Janice, had separated and were divorcing. Janice became convinced Isaac was having an affair with a mutual friend, Kate. I tried not to pry into any of this, but I recalled running into Isaac and Kate at the movie theater a year earlier when I saw *Fantastic Four*. Now that moment made sense to me. I had a hard time warming up to Kate since I viewed her as a possible homewrecker and I wasn't entirely sure what to think of Isaac either. Regardless, Issac and Janice were now embroiled in a bitter divorce and custody battle over their four-year-old daughter, Megan. Memorizing my script was the least of his worries.

We were going to film a scene from the chapter of the script entitled "The Sub Par Hitmen." I wrote the script in chapters, occasionally out of sequence, as an homage to Quentin Tarantino. Jimmy showed up and was ready to go. He was thin, had shoulder-length black hair, and wore black attire. He looked like a younger version of Trent Reznor. Eric and I tied up Isaac and Jimmy in the basement, a legit creepy place to film this scene. One dilemma was a lack of chairs, so they had to sit on the floor. The rope was also flimsy and barely tied them together. I placed a saw nearby that was supposed to be out of reach. In reality, Isaac could have easily reached the saw and cut the rope.

The shoot itself quickly turned into a disaster. It was so bad it was hilariously funny. The dialogue I found edgy and cool in high school didn't work, so I told Isaac to put it in his own words. The problem was he couldn't remember *any* of the lines, and the ones he remembered came out stilted and comical.

Some of the highlights included: "There was a woman with them. They were both raping her!" This was supposed to be an intense, painful memory, but was laugh-out-loud funny with Isaac's delivery.

Another "great" moment was a wide-eyed Isaac saying, "They could have shot my ass, but they didn't. They just opened the door and left."

Or how about: "I ran out of the house to the church next door. Don't ask me why. When you're as stoned as I was, you don't exactly know what you're doing." His delivery of the line cracked up both Eric and me. The one thing I will say about Jimmy is no matter how hysterically bad things got, he never broke character and never burst out laughing.

The entire shoot was a catastrophe. I met up with Jimmy sometime later at his house near Iroquois Park to edit this mess into something coherent with Final Cut Pro. There was about nine minutes of actual footage, and maybe three turned out to be usable. Clearly I had these guys in the exact wrong roles. A few days later, I showed the unedited footage to Chad, who of course howled with laughter joking, "Why did you put Isaac in this role? This other guy Jimmy looks much more like a crackhead!"

I took a step back to reassess the situation. I convinced Jimmy to be in this thing because I told him he didn't have to memorize much dialogue, but now I needed to convince him to tackle the much more difficult role of Brad. Sure enough, he agreed without much prodding. I almost wonder if he wanted to do it, realizing he was the more obvious fit for the role.

After several weeks, I managed to corral everyone back at Isaac's house to refilm scene. The shoot went much better for a variety of reasons. First, I brought chairs. Second, I figured out the camera and used the orange tinted filter to give the basement the feeling of being hell on earth. We discarded the goofy saw and used more rope. Most importantly, Jimmy was much better as Brad. Isaac still had some occasional lines as Chris that sounded odd, but overall, he was better than the first attempt. In the words of Groucho Marx, "We worked our way up from nothing to a case of extreme poverty."

In the following weeks, we filmed more scenes. I tried anything that didn't require anyone else. We filmed a scene outside an abandoned Chevron near my apartment where Brad and Chris discussed the antics of legendary punk rock lunatic GG Allin. We also went to the abandoned U of L daycare (where I met both Isaac and Chad as kids). As long as a permit wasn't necessary, we filmed in settings that were the Ghosts of Louisville Past. I filmed some other Brad/Chris scenes in cars, as well as a key moment of Brad throwing his drug stash in a garbage can in Iroquois Park. We used my apartment for some scenes of exposition, as well as a wacky new scene I wrote where the heroes discuss the ill-fated Image/Valiant crossover, *Deathmate*. Some of the scenes were amusing enough, even intentionally so, as Isaac and Jimmy developed some rapport. Isaac was a poor man's Jason Lee, a vibe which worked better in these scenes.

We filmed on and off for most of the summer. Before anything else could be done, I became preoccupied with something more important. In early September, I received a cease-and-desist letter from a lawyer in Los Angeles representing Warner Bros. and Turner Classic Movies listing titles from my website that were their properties. Curiously, they left out the RKO titles, showing not even Turner's own people cared about the RKO library. I understood their rationale, but nothing I listed was commercially available. (Warner Archive wouldn't be a reality until 2009.)

I went into an absolute panic. On occasion, eBay tossed a listing, or I might have an occasional idiot whine to PayPal, but this was potentially a disaster. I responded that, to my knowledge, nothing I offered was currently available commercially or was public domain. I would be glad to remove the titles from my site. The move harmed my site, but it satisfied the lawyer. A final letter informed me they wouldn't pursue the matter. The scare convinced me to keep applying to schools so I could do something else besides sell bootlegs.

I kept messing around with *Welcome to Paradise* into the fall, but I needed some female leads and had no idea who would want to tackle any of these parts for no money. The role of Sally would be tough. The character was a highly sexualized but intelligent prostitute. Michaela was the ill-fated gangster's moll who Brad described being horribly raped and murdered. Jennifer Lawrence would knock either role out of the park today, but she was about sixteen then. I figured Rosie, Brad's bi-curious girlfriend, would be the easiest role to cast.

Jimmy recommended a girl named Shannon who lived at Tanglewood Apartments right near me. I went to her apartment on a Saturday afternoon and showed her the script. She was a rail-thin goth chick. Shannon put on *The Downward Spiral*, and as "Mr. Self-Destruct" was playing, read over the scene I wanted her to do. When she finished, she turned to me and said, "Okay, cool. I understand Rosie. I can do this."

About a week later, we filmed the Brad/Rosie scene at Shannon's apartment. It was a key scene where Rosie confesses to Brad she paid for Sally's services as a prostitute. For whatever reason, I wasn't feeling it. Maybe due to a lack of chemistry or the dreary lighting, but I didn't find the scene memorable, even in a bad way. Between takes I made sure to check the score of the U of L/Cincinnati football game, which the Cards won 23-17, running their record to 6-0 in what was shaping up to be a dream season. When we finished, Jimmy said, "I don't know when you want to edit this, but I'll be busy at work for the next few days."

"Duly noted," I replied. I don't think we ever got together again. Although we still keep in touch on Facebook, that was the last time I saw Jimmy.

In truth, my enthusiasm was waning. I appreciated everyone who volunteered, but there was one inescapable fact—the footage was amateur hour stuff. The script was too ambitious and needed professional actors. Where was I going to film the subway scenes? I needed to have a producer, or at least a production manager. The fatal flaw was a lack of actual planning. We were building a plane while trying to fly it. Maybe Chad was right when he suggested, "You need to write something like *Clerks* that you can film at a store or wherever. Something with a couple of locations and a few actors."

Whatever momentum the project had vanished one day in mid-October. I hopped online to check my eBay listings when Kate messaged me on AIM. She was freaking out over something to do with Isaac.

"Brian, can you give me a ride? I don't have a car at the moment and I am worried about Isaac. He's at his dad's house but isn't picking up the phone."

"Is this a big deal? Maybe he's in the shower or something," I replied.

"Isaac has been feeling depressed lately with all that has been going on. Last night I walked two miles in the rain to his friend's house to check on him at three a.m."

"So are you worried he is going to do something to himself?"

"I don't know. Maybe. Can you pick me up and take me to his dad's house?"

I agreed to come pick her up at her cousin's house in Okolona. I couldn't decide if Kate's gesture was romantic or just plain looney. Either way, I picked her up and we headed to Isaac's house. Kate was a couple of months older than me, a heavy-set woman with some patches of hair on her chin she later had removed or waxed.

I didn't know what to expect when we walked in. Kate had me worried we might find Isaac in the bathtub with his wrists slashed. He was sitting on the bed, ready to head to work at UPS. His phone had either died, or he turned it off.

"Hey, man. You doing okay? Kate's been worried."

"Yeah, I'm getting ready to go to work."

If something was bothering him, he wasn't willing to talk about it with me. Soon after, I left the room and let Kate talk to him for a while. I was puzzled by the whole situation, and uncomfortable being dragged into whatever was going on. Their awkward conversation revealed no new details, and after a few minutes, Kate was ready to leave. What the hell? As we approached my car, Kate asked, "Can you take me to Audubon Hospital? I need to see a sick relative."

"Kate, you really need a car," I replied. I was never quite sure who she visited, but after that, we headed back to her cousin's house.

"I'm sorry to put you through all this today. Why don't you come inside and have a drink?" she offered. There were a bunch of kids inside she had to watch; I believe they belonged to her cousin. In between Kate yelling at them, the topic turned to the film project. I brought a

DVD of the initial unedited footage with me, so I put it on, and we laughed uproariously at Isaac's riveting performance. That was my first bonding experience with Kate, and while I still didn't especially want her around, I could see she cared about Isaac more than his ex-wife ever had.

After that day, I pulled the plug on filming *Welcome to Paradise*. The project wasn't going anywhere. Isaac had too many things going on in his private life to keep filming. Jimmy had his own projects. Chad was off the rails and remained that way until a freak aneurysm nearly killed him in 2007 and he cleaned up his act.

Welcome to Paradise had been a bust and I was back to square one. Back to applying to more schools. Back to going over to my mom's house at night to make sure my brother went to school in the morning. Back to helping my dad get in and out of bed and changing his TV channel at four a.m. Filmmaking is more difficult than I figured it would be. I had a new respect for those who do it, even if I didn't always enjoy their efforts. It's such a torment to have ideas in your head you can't figure out how to execute. It is the sort of thing that can drive someone crazy.

Alas, U of L's epic football dream season fell barely short. A week after one of the greatest wins in school history over West Virginia, the Cards had to go on the road to face unbeaten Rutgers. U of L jumped out to a 25-7 lead in the first half, but Rutgers shut the Cardinals out in the second half and hit a last second field goal to win 28-25. All U of L had to do was win that game to stay #3 in the country and wait for the winner of Michigan/Ohio State. That night, I was so upset about the loss I couldn't sleep. U of L still finished 12-1 and won the Orange Bowl, but 2006 was the one chance U of L ever had at winning a football national championship. The Louisville/Rutgers game was voted Game of the Year on ESPN. It remains the worst I've ever felt about a single sporting event. The next morning's *Courier-Journal* headline read "The dream slips away" in huge, bold letters.

One morning in late 2006, I was over at my mom's again, my brother off at school, and I was having breakfast with my parents. My dad asked, "What is your plan now? What are you going to do?" I didn't know how to respond, but finally answered.

"I might try applying to USC. I also think Southern Illinois has some kind of film and TV program. I have been looking at UNC Greensboro as well. I guess I could also try FSU again since I was an alternate there. At least I have a highlight reel for a portfolio with the stuff we filmed."

"At some point you need to quit bothering with all of this and get a real job," my mom said. She was probably right, but I had a vision of what I wanted to do and wasn't ready to give up. Not yet.

As I drove back to my apartment on that rainy, overcast morning, all of the events of the past year seemed to hit me at once. My frustrations and failures, the periodic meltdowns, my friends and their problems, everything. I was on the verge of tears as I drove past Fairdale High School on the Gene Snyder Freeway. I started flipping through radio stations and settled on an oldies station. "Rose Garden" by Lynn Anderson was playing. I had heard the song before, but that was the first time it connected with me. As I stared out at the road ahead, trying to stay composed, I kept hearing the chorus of the song in my head. The song stayed with me until I reached my apartment.

CHAPTER 7

CLIFTON OAKS

By mid-2009, I found myself at a crossroads. I shut down my website, Cabbageboy Movies since the writing was on the wall for quite some time. The economy was in the toilet after the 2008 financial meltdown and it was time to make a change.

All of my attempts to start film school had either failed or were so laughably costly I would have had to put my mom's house up as collateral. I attempted to start another site selling car radars, but I knew nothing about them, and to be honest, my heart wasn't in it. The communication department at U of L had started the Master of Arts program the preceding year, so with few options, I decided to apply. I was admitted easily enough and started graduate school in August 2009.

Truth be told, I had more on my mind than grad school. The long-running situation with my dad hit a critical point in 2009 when my mom fell and broke her leg that October. Since she couldn't deal with my dad while she was ailing, it fell on Eric to deal with him since I was now busy with grad school. My mom was doing physical rehab and Eric couldn't deal with my dad full-time. We agreed it was time to put my dad in a nursing home. My mom shifted money to my brother's bank account and we figured out how to apply for Medicaid.

My mom fell again in December 2009, on the ramp at the house while trying to bring in some food from the store. At least Eric and I were also there carrying bags, so we were able to brace her fall. As she sat there, I could tell she was at the end of her rope.

With tears in her eyes, she said, "I need a divorce." Soon after, she filed the paperwork with a lawyer. It was the most feasible thing that could have been done since there was no viable way to put my dad in a nursing home while they were still married. Since the house was in her name, the state couldn't touch it. All other assets, however, could only be protected if they were divorced and nothing was in my dad's name. Otherwise those assets would be fair game for the nursing home or being counted as part of a Medicaid penalty period.

In essence, what originally was a divorce filed for technical legal reasons became a much more legitimate one filled with vitriol. My dad felt horribly upset and during his last few months at home, he became more and more impossible. In fact, he was flat-out vile to be around, verbally abusive, and at one point refused to sign the divorce papers. Eventually, he relented, realizing that after all of his verbally abusive behavior, none of us even wanted him around.

My dad's half-brother, Monty, who lived in Florida, called me during all the turmoil. He had heard about the divorce and called me to rant about how his brother was being treated. "How is this fair at all? Kentucky law states he is due fifty percent of all assets. He should get part of that house!"

"Monty, he can't get anything. That's the point. He can't have half ownership in the house, or bank account, or car, or anything."

"Then he's being screwed here. I have half a mind to come up there and intervene myself."

I was trying to be patient, but it was an insane conversation.

"Look, he's going into a nursing home. We have to protect our assets or else the state is going to take everything. I'm not sure why you can't grasp this concept."

"But he should get half of that house—"

Eventually, I hung up on him. I was at my wit's end and refused to hear any more of his nonsense. Monty's wife, Merrie, sent me a message on Facebook apologizing for his rant, but I never spoke to him again. Monty died of a heart attack in 2017, and I sometimes regret the last conversation we ever had.

Dad claimed the whole situation "was embarrassing for the neighbors" and other absurd statements designed to delay the inevitable. His rants were now on the level of Mel Gibson's domestic craziness, but eventually, he signed the divorce papers.

My dad entered Clifton Oaks Care Center in March 2010. The nursing home was a long drive from my mom's house, but it was the only place she could find that had an available Medicaid bed. His last night at home was a Sunday, and we let him watch whatever movie he wanted. His pick was *Shane*, one of his all-time favorite westerns. As Little Joey kept pleading, "Come back, Shane!" near the end of the film, I looked over and saw my dad in tears. I was practically in tears myself.

"Are you coming over tomorrow?" he asked, trying to compose himself.

"I don't know. Probably," I replied, also trying to compose myself.

"I guess I won't be here." And he wasn't.

There are some instances in life where there aren't easy answers, and this was one of them. Late 2009 and early 2010 was a difficult time for my family. Sending my dad to the nursing home felt tantamount to issuing him a death sentence. As we tried to assure ourselves, what else could we do?

PART TWO

WELCOME TO DEBATE

CHAPTER 8

REBELS WITH A CAUSE

I must confess, before August 2009, I never thought much of debate beyond whatever I saw on TV. I don't even remember if Butler Traditional High School had a debate team at all, and the activity never crossed my radar as an undergrad. I will freely admit hearing about a graduate assistantship with the University of Louisville's Malcolm X Debate Team gave me pause. As a white male, I was unsure of whether I should apply, but I went ahead and did so upon the urging of my advisor, Dr. Janet Gregory. A few weeks later, the phone rang.

"Hello, Brian. This is Marlene Mayhew from the Malcolm X Debate Team. Our first choice for the graduate assistant role had to back out due to not having a valid driver's license. We travel to tourneys, after all. So, we are going to offer you the position." Upon hearing this news, I raced down to Davidson Hall before anyone with the team could change their mind. Marlene, a middle aged white woman, handed me the paperwork and I gladly signed it. I went from looking at serious student loan debt to having paid tuition and $1,200 a month in the blink of an eye.

The U of L debate program was in a state of chaos as I entered it. Dr. Kendall Bedford, Director of Debate, had been arrested in

July 2009 due to a domestic incident with his wife, and as a result, his status was unclear. In fact, Bedford wasn't allowed to participate in the team's retreat in mid-August. The relevance of this situation would have a deep and lasting impact on the team going forward. I vaguely remembered Dr. Bedford from my undergrad days. He was a tall, bald Black man and definitely could be an intimidating presence.

My role as a graduate assistant wasn't clearly defined. Program Assistant Marlene Mayhew knew of my web-building experience, so managing the team's website wound up being my responsibility. In addition to the tech end, I also actively participated in the team's meetings and had to write all of the speeches that the team members also wrote and delivered, at least initially.

The first day of the retreat was like walking into a completely foreign culture. With Dr. Bedford suspended, Program Coordinator Brittany Pollard dictated the proceedings. She discussed the resolution for the 2009–10 year, which was, "The United States Government should reduce the amount or role of its nuclear weapons arsenal."

Our initial assignments involved reading a series of Dr. Bedford's blog postings. These postings didn't relate in any way, shape, or form to the topic of the year's debates, but instead dealt with the "untold story" of Dr. Bedford's arrest. The details now are inconsequential, but the notion we would take time out of our debate retreat to discuss this completely baffled me. One first-year debater, Kyle Resnick, took major issue with having to read Dr. Bedford's blog, a preview of upcoming clashes to come.

During the course of the retreat, the squad discussed the idea of using debate to create social change, and at one point in a discussion, Pollard (hereby known as Bubo, a nickname taken from the wacky owl in her favorite movie, *Clash of the Titans*) asked me point blank, "Do you feel as though you have the agency to make a change?"

I had never been asked such a question before, so I paused for a moment and then answered, "Uh...sure." In addition to Dr. Bedford's personal blog posts, we also had to write and deliver a series of speeches that later tied into our actual debate strategy. I was never sure why I needed to do these speeches beyond a basic introductory speech.

Here is a confession: I am a lousy public speaker. I am usually nervous and don't feel comfortable having to deliver a speech, so needless to say, I dug deep to muster up the nerve to deliver speeches in the debate room about my unconditional love of debate or my purpose in debate. Other speeches included one about finding balance in life and debate, another on unconditional love, and an uncomfortable speech about addicts and enablers where I relayed a story about the time I realized a lifelong friend had been using cocaine. I gave several other speeches as well, including one on my vision of debate, having a sense of agency, and others. I had no idea how this process related to debate, but I got into a solid rhythm of writing and delivering these speeches and most of them seemed to go over well with staff and debaters alike.

These speeches lasted the first few weeks of the Fall '09 semester, with bits and pieces forming the basis for each debater's 1AC (1st Affirmative Constructive in a debate). The second portion of the strategy came into effect, which started to make more sense. The next series of three-minute speeches consisted of discussions of representative democracy, which included the roles of constituents, advocates, and decision-makers.

The team was going to pick a constituent on both sides of the nuclear weapons issue and advocate on their behalf. Most of the debaters didn't seem to grasp the fluidity of these concepts, which was an ominous sign of things to come. (Someone can drift from decision-maker to constituent.) At first, there was a speech discussing these three groups in our private lives, then a segue into discussion of these roles in terms of government policymaking. For instance, lobbyists act as advocates for their particular constituents and influence decision-makers in Washington. The idea was to become advocates on the behalf anti-nuclear weapons activists.

A memorable squad meeting occurred in September 2009, one that resonates with me even today. Dr. Bedford discussed the norms and procedures of debate, a list Bedford noted are rampantly abused in the realm of policy debate. The most horrific norm to me was the use of extreme speed. To illustrate this point, squad newcomers had to watch the 2004 National Debate Tournament documentary, the last time U of L had much success. I was appalled. All I saw was a bunch of people spewing down at seemingly 400 words per minute. Whatever reticence I had about our strategy went out the window when I saw this video. If we opposed this type of debate, great.

The critiques of speed would be a constant for the entire year; whenever a team used speed, our teams would use it against them. This was a clincher for me. We were right about at least some of these norms. However, as I now realize, learning these norms and procedures and having a firm grasp of them would have been beneficial, even if the team had no desire to use them.

Another taboo strategy to Dr. Bedford was the use of permutations. A permutation goes like this in debate: Team A proposes a plan, and then Team B proposes a counter plan. Team A counters by saying, "We can do both plans since they aren't mutually exclusive." U of L stubbornly refused to execute a permutation, even when one made sense, thinking, "We can do our plan and your plan too" is tantamount to plagiarism. I always felt this was a mistake since permutations were clearly allowed by all judges and tournaments, and in my two years with the team, we never had a solid answer for why someone couldn't perm us.

In order to execute our constituents/advocates/decision-maker strategy, we needed to find a constituent on the affirmative and the negative. This negative constituent proved to be a massive problem. The affirmative constituent proved easy to find. I picked an umbrella group of nuclear activists called the Nuclear Weapons Complex Consolidation Policy Network and we planned to advocate on behalf of them.

The dilemma was finding someone who opposed the resolution. How on earth could a social activist debate team advocate on behalf of a government agency such as the National Nuclear Security Administration, the sort of people our affirmative constituents opposed? Regardless, we settled on the NNSA as our negative constituent.

Our cross-examination strategy was to ask questions such as, "Who is your constituent? What do they represent? How can you ethically represent these people?" The dilemma to me personally was how we ethically represent these constituents if we hadn't contacted them or asked for permission? I talked to some of the activists for a separate class paper, but to my knowledge no one ever contacted anyone at the NNSA. Resnick in particular took issue with the NNSA as a constituent, asking, "Should we be doing this, advocating on the behalf of a possibly corrupt government agency?"

The strategy came along so slowly the planned trip to Atlanta for the Georgia State tournament was canceled. The aforementioned Kyle Resnick argued repeatedly with Dr. Bedford to the point where Resnick quit the team, and veteran debater John Williams's personal problems led to him being AWOL for much of the Fall '09 semester. Essentially, the entire month had been a process of setting up a nine-minute 1AC and nine-minute 1NC (affirmative and negative constructive).

The beginning of the end for Resnick was when he gave a curious speech downplaying nuclear weapons in general, saying, "No one in the world wants to seriously use nuclear weapons." I happened to be giving a speech next and my already prepared speech mentioned potentially threatening nations such as Iran and North Korea.

"Good grief, Kyle! Brian accidentally countered your argument—with evidence!" Dr. Bedford replied indignantly.

I ran into Resnick a week later outside Davidson Hall. We talked briefly about his time on the debate team and what went wrong.

"So, what happened with you, man?" I asked. "Why did you quit the team?"

"I couldn't do it anymore," he replied. "I kept arguing with Dr. Bedford every meeting and things weren't working out. He upset me too much, so it was time to leave."

On a personal level, I still had no idea how to judge a debate. In fact, I didn't know anything about the actual structure of a debate until right before we left for the UNLV tournament in Las Vegas. The framework goes as thus:

1AC (First affirmative constructive, nine minutes), three minutes of cross examination, 1NC (first negative constructive, nine minutes), three minutes of cross ex, 2AC (second affirmative constructive, nine minutes), three minutes of cross ex, 2NC (second negative constructive, nine minutes), three minutes of cross ex. The constructive speeches are then followed by the six-minute rebuttals: 1NR (first negative rebuttal, which combined with the 2NC constitutes the negative "block"), 1AR (first affirmative rebuttal), 2NR (second negative rebuttal), and finally the 2AR (second affirmative rebuttal). Each team had a total of ten minutes of prep time to prepare speeches. If all that sounds hard to grasp, imagine being told this format for the first time and then being expected to judge debates a few days later.

All of this was a baffling culture shock to me. First, I will admit the racially-charged nature of our program made me somewhat uncomfortable. When I told my parents about the team, my dad quipped, "Is this professor of yours stuck in the '60s?" Second, the curious use of music by our debaters struck me as counterproductive and made me wonder if it was a waste of valuable speaking time, since judges might not take note of the songs (Lauryn Hill, Sam Cooke, several others). Cooke's "A Change Is Gonna Come" was the ideal song choice for our philosophy. Lastly, not only was our approach completely foreign to me, but the so called "traditional" debate teams didn't seem traditional either. No one debated the way one would see it on television.

Thus, what few teams we had managed to cobble something together by the time we went to Las Vegas in early October. Williams was not prepared to debate since he had missed so much squad. The varsity teams consisted of returning debaters Carl Vance and Miriam Bouvier; veteran debater Vicky McDonald and newcomer Natalie Abercrombie (who should have been in novice with Resnick but was shoehorned in); and the novice newcomer team of Darren Mathers and Keisha Fisher. For reference's sake, Vance was the lone white debater on the team during the first year I spent with the program. Josie Jefferson was granted another semester of eligibility and became Williams's partner in the spring.

For the time being, Dr. Bedford took me under his wing. I sat beside him on the plane to Vegas. We had our own informal debate of who was better between the 1990s Bulls or the 1980s Lakers and Celtics.

"I would say the best teams in NBA history would have to be the 1980s Lakers or Celtics. Too many offensive options for the Jordan Bulls to cover," he said.

"I will take the 1996 Bulls," I replied. "Their Pythagorean win/loss numbers are better than any of the Lakers or Celtics teams from the '80s. Better defense too. Now the 1972 Lakers vs. the 1996 Bulls? There's an interesting matchup."

"You know, I forgot about that Lakers team. An interesting hypothetical matchup, to be sure," he said.

We even roomed together for a while on the trip, even though Dr. Bedford had a university chaperone (Dr. Thomas, a Black female Pan-African Studies professor) as part of his probation agreement. Eventually Dr. Thomas left and went back to Louisville, and I took her room. By the last day, Dr. Bedford had tired of rooming with me. He felt I took too long in the shower.

I judged quite often in Vegas at the UNLV tournament and tried to make sense of it as best I could. I judged novice rounds, so the speed aspect didn't factor into things. Primarily, I judged Weber State novice debates, lots of God-awful Weber State novice debates. Sometimes the Weber kids agreed with the other team out of the box, and then ranted about the lameness of the other team's plan. One team countered their own plan from the 1AC with their 2AC. This was a complete mess. This sucked. I wanted to go home. I was tired of judging this junk.

On the second day, I went off on one Weber State team for using what I later realized to be a permutation, but in my notes, I wrote down as an "outrageous shift in advocacy." In reality, they had done nothing wrong by stating, "We can do both plans." By the end of the tourney, I had judged four Weber St. debates, and they went 0–4 in those rounds. I heard through the grapevine their debaters hated me and thought I was unethical. Weber State's team was so downtrodden they didn't bother to show up at the closing ceremony.

In a later conversation with Dr. Bedford, I remarked that I didn't care what Weber State thinks, to which he responded, "I do. We are trying to build coalitions." I never grasped the idea of trying to build coalitions in a competitive activity, especially when our style of debate was so confrontational. At least I didn't understand the concept my first year with the team.

Mathers and Fisher put together enough wins to stagger into the elimination rounds at 3–4. The varsity teams fared even worse, with Vance/Bouvier going 2–5 and McDonald/Abercrombie going 1–4. They sat out the last couple of rounds since Bubo and Dr. Bedford didn't want to crush Natalie's psyche.

We won some debates on the affirmative, but the negative posed a major problem. Judge after judge couldn't bring themselves to vote for a team advocating on behalf of "evil" government agencies like the NNSA. I voiced my concerns beforehand to little avail. Dr. Bedford instructed everyone to drop the NNSA as a constituent mid-tourney. We tried to have a negative strategy with no actual constituent, leading to repeated rambling about spreading "effective decision-making in a multicultural democracy." Sometimes we asked the other team if they had a constituent, while we didn't have one ourselves. This too was a mess.

Mathers/Fisher faced Cal State Fullerton in the elims but lost on a 3–0 count (elimination rounds have three judges). Our novice duo was getting by purely on speaking skill and bravado. They had no clue how to execute a cross ex and no idea how to execute rebuttals either. The strategy of using one-third personal narrative, one-third setup for our constituent, and one-third topical plan was too flawed to work, especially with the NNSA as the negative constituent. Furthermore, the first third of the speech with personal narrative didn't link with the rest of the speech. What did Darren Mathers's narrative about a harrowing childhood experience with his parents have to do with the NWCCPN? What did Vicky McDonald's narrative about fighting with another girl over a boy have to do with nukes? These speeches were the same sort of disconnected evidence we criticized other teams for using.

The Vegas trip was not a total loss, however. We spent one night out on the strip, where I went with Dr. Bedford and his cousin (a Vegas resident) to the Venetian for the big Vikings/Packers game. I laid down $20 on the Vikings at -6.5. Minnesota won 30–23, as Brett Favre defeated his former team, so I won the bet. After the game, I ventured out onto the strip with some of the debaters, but I couldn't do much in Vegas with a bunch of college kids who were mostly under twenty-one. After walking the strip, I took the tram and went back to our off-strip Best Western. This was my first time in Vegas, and I should have brought a better jacket since the desert got cold at night in early October.

Two weeks later, we set back out on the road to Nashville for the Vanderbilt tournament. There were a few adjustments made in the strategy, but the warning signs became apparent. The main difference involved the type of teams making up the Vanderbilt field compared to the Vegas field. Most of the western teams were laid-back critique teams, more performance oriented. The field at Vanderbilt consisted of flat-out policy debate with a few exceptions, such as West Georgia. West Georgia was theoretically an ally, but personally I found the whole gendered language critique strategy little more than being the Word Police. They were always thrilled to go after the slightest gendered infraction.

Since I didn't observe Abercrombie and McDonald in Vegas, I made sure to check out two of their debates. I monitored one with Emory and the another against West Georgia. The Emory debate left me stunned as to what our squad was doing strategy-wise. Emory's affirmative put forth a plan that the United States should join in a multilateral agreement to ratify the Comprehensive Test Ban Treaty in order to aide Native Americans in the Southwest. By now, our negative constituent was to invoke the legacy of U of L debaters past, a baffling strategy which didn't yield great results since it put past U of L debaters into the position of the NNSA as a constituent.

One problem worried me from the previous tourney. We simply didn't answer *any* arguments from the other team. In this case, the counter was simple. The United States didn't need to enter a multilateral agreement to stop abusing Native Americans, but instead the USA could adopt a unilateral approach. Judge George Patterson saw the exact same debate I did, so I wasn't crazy. The complete lack of addressing arguments was in fact a part of our strategy. As Dr. Bedford exclaimed in a squad meeting, "When we were at our best it didn't matter what our opponents did. It mattered what we did!"

I watched a second debate with Abercrombie and McDonald immediately after the first. I was even more horrified by what I saw. At one point in this round against West Georgia, Vicky McDonald addressed our opponents' use of speed and said, "When you do that you take my partner out of the round. She is a first-year debater, and you are making her invisible." I couldn't believe we noted the inexperience of a debater during a round. I was stunned to hear from the duo after the round that Bubo instructed them to make such an argument.

"Wait, Bubo *told* you to inform the judge Natalie sucks as a debater? Because that's what I heard," I said.

As I would later understand, the argument they attempted was based on Ralph Ellison's *Invisible Man*. The problem is they never specifically mentioned Ellison's book by name, so the argument came off like, "Hey, you took my partner out of the round, meanie." Is this not a good thing to do in order to win a debate?

At least I escaped from the madness and judged debates on the second day of the tourney. This was where I got my first look at the most dominant novice debate program in the country: Liberty. In round after round, I saw Liberty teams overwhelm inexperienced novice opponents with mounds of evidence and arguments. On an amusing note, Darren Mathers later told me he and Keisha Fisher ran into a Liberty team in a previous round where the cocky Liberty guy asked, "How are you doing in the tourney? We're 4–0." Mathers's response: "You're about to be 4–1." Once again, the novices succeeded in this tourney, going 4–2 and making the elim rounds. Unfortunately, they lost to another Liberty team in an elim round since the initial Liberty team scouted our entire strategy.

The other two teams were a disaster. Bouvier and Vance went 0–6, losing every debate and having heated verbal altercations with judges and debaters. McDonald and Abercrombie weren't much better (1–5). The most notorious debate featured Bouvier and Vance with Liberty coach Hazel Ball presiding as judge.

In her summation, Ball stated, "If you are really so unhappy with the state of the debate community, why don't you just leave?"

"Her idea for change in the debate community was for us to get out of it," Bubo ranted. "Back to Africa, bitch! She may as well have said that."

There were nightmarish stories of other teams treating our debaters with no respect, snatching papers out of our hands, and cussing us out during debate rounds.

Since I was judging the second day, I didn't see much of this abuse, so I took everyone's word for it. My lack of direct experience with these unpleasant events left me perplexed at the direction the team was about to take. I had only seen two of our rounds, judged a ton of other rounds, and hadn't personally seen much of anything wrong. In retrospect, we had such a bad initial strategy I wondered if Dr. Bedford wanted to dehumanize the team and start to do the strategy he really wanted. I ventured back to Louisville that Sunday, since I had a communication department orientation class to attend, so I missed out on whatever vitriol was unleashed during Darren and Keisha's elim round.

The first squad meeting after the Vanderbilt tourney was a watershed moment for my involvement with team strategy. Dr. Bedford went on one of his usual tirades, in particular on Hazel Ball, ranting, "These judges like Hazel Ball told you all to leave, to get out of the community! You have to tell her 'Fuck you, bitch! You leave! You get out of the community because we're staying!'" After the tirade, he asked everyone for their opinions, and I felt the need to speak up.

"I saw a couple of our debates and I don't think we're doing a very good job of answering the other team's arguments," I said.

"Yeah, well I know about your views of debate. I spent a weekend with you in Vegas," he replied in flippant fashion, referring back to my dismissal of Weber State. Then he proceeded to move on to a new piece of business.

I didn't want to let the issue die, however. After squad, I walked over to Bubo's desk where she was conversing with Dr. Bedford and elaborated on my views, in particular the two Abercrombie/McDonald debates I saw in Nashville. I mentioned how stunned I was at what I perceived as McDonald inadvertently throwing Abercrombie under the bus, making her inexperience known to the room. They asked what I would have said in the judge's place, to which I replied, "I would have said 'You know, maybe you need to be in novice rounds with other first-year debaters.' I assume Natalie was supposed to team with Kyle in the novice division?"

"I don't want to have this discussion with you right now," Dr. Bedford replied. With that statement, I shrugged my shoulders and walked away.

After the Vanderbilt fiasco, Dr. Bedford made the decision to go in a much different and radical direction, namely one of pure protest. No more Mister Nice Guy. No more letting other teams kick us around. No more topical discussion whatsoever. All of the material I came up with in regard to the NWCCPN was tossed aside in favor of a flat-out protest of the debate community. This strategy was not what I signed up for. I wanted to help research the topic at hand, to figure out a strategy that would work in terms of nuclear weapons policy. When the team went in the direction of total protest, I felt disenfranchised.

As far as the team goes, no one asked me what I thought for the next two months. I never spoke to anyone involved with the team other than Marlene Mayhew. I became one of the marginalized voices the team spoke about in debates. In essence, I became invisible. Dr.

Bedford railed against groupthink in the debate community yet seemed oblivious to the groupthink in his own program.

Since we were moving in a totally new direction, the planned trip to Wake Forest was canceled, with debaters being given the assignment of writing four entirely new speeches. The rationale according to Dr. Bedford: "We will protest the white privileged forms of competition in the ADA (American Debate Association), AFA (American Forensics Association), and CEDA (Cross Examination Debate Association). Everyone should look at their rules and guidelines and then come up with new speeches. Until we feel safe in the community, we will protest. Until they uphold their own written documents, we will protest."

Indeed, these new speeches were meant to intentionally create disturbances at tournaments, disrupt the other teams, and make the judges highly uncomfortable. They would raise questions about the nature of policy debate and insist that to be a party to it was to be implicated. I found the strategy to be insane, but since I was being paid to be there, I didn't raise a fuss and cashed the paycheck.

As part of this new strategy, no one was allowed to ask or answer any cross-ex questions at the next tournament. When another team asked us questions, our duos would respond with quotes from the Denzel Washington film *The Great Debaters*: "Who is the judge? The judge is God. Who is my opponent? He doesn't exist but is only a dissenting voice to the truth that I speak." Dr. Bedford pondered why the film wasn't a hit, and after watching it, I thought the Depression era setting was too long ago for civil rights–oriented filmmaking, and that the film lacked any sort of white ally characters. Whites in the film were either racist rednecks or white privileged debaters.

In addition to the Ellison book, there were several other pieces of evidence introduced for the new strategy. For the white privilege argument, everyone turned to Peggy McIntosh's *Unpacking the Invisible Knapsack* for an entire list of privileges that whites have in society constituting "an invisible knapsack of unearned assets."

Furthermore, everyone started employing Tim Wise's evidence on debate: "Debate from my own experiences is very, very white. It appeals to the way white folks think with its speed reading and constant nuclear holocaust scenarios rather than real-world views. It is nothing but high-speed mental masturbation." Of the new evidence, I could relate to Wise the most. Not only are advanced-level debaters speed crazy, but the constant use of nuclear holocaust scenarios borders on self-parody. At least with this particular resolution, the use of nuclear war made sense. When people discuss nuclear annihilation in a debate on immigration reform, this strategy becomes laughable.

There were several hopeful end results of the strategy. First, we were going to make the governing bodies of the ADA, AFA, and CEDA uphold their own mission statements. Second, this action would render U of L visible again in the debate community. I feared we wouldn't win one round doing this strategy. How could a debate team possibly win any rounds if they are not discussing the topic? I agreed the initial strategy wasn't working but wasn't sure if we could fix it this way. I had an ominous feeling as the team adjourned for the winter break. Things couldn't become any more dysfunctional than they already had been, could they?

CHAPTER 9

A TIME FOR PROTEST

One significant development happened during the team's January retreat. The decision was made to enter the tourney at Navy. We planned to drive to Annapolis in the middle of January, through the mountains of Eastern Kentucky and West Virginia. Furthermore, we weren't going there merely to debate, but rather to "protest" the debate community at one of the most hardcore policy-oriented tourneys. I would like to say I second-guessed this idea, but in reality, I first-guessed it. Dr. Bedford said the day before the trip, "Everyone get in the van tomorrow morning. Something special will happen. I don't know what that will be yet, but something special will happen."

The Navy trip was such a complete disaster it's difficult to comprehend unless you were actually there. It was a terrifying experience that nearly tore apart the Louisville debate program. The tournament had lasting ramifications being felt to this day. The trip there took fourteen hours since we ran into a terrible snow and ice storm somewhere in rural West Virginia. We navigated the trip between Charleston and Morgantown on roads that were barely there. I would have been terrified had I not been so utterly exhausted. We arrived in Annapolis at

2:30 a.m. and crashed in our rooms. Thankfully, the tourney didn't begin until 5:00 p.m. so there was time to rest. Regardless, this sort of excruciating trip cannot possibly lead to good debating.

Adding to the protest nature of the strategy, Dr. Bedford had an explanation printed up for judges discussing the nature of the protest. I now had a new judging philosophy; one I had no hand in writing. It dealt with voting for the team that best upheld the ADA/CEDA constitutions, and best adhered to an all-inclusive form of debate. I was still becoming acclimated to being a judge in the first place. Having to follow a head-scratching new philosophy was the last thing I needed, since I didn't have a firm grasp of the new philosophy and teams started deviating from their usual strategies to acquiesce to my "demands."

I vividly recall the first round of the tourney. John Williams was now back in the good graces of the team and debating, and Josie Jefferson stepped in for one final semester of debating to be his partner. Jefferson was essentially a player-coach and clearly the best debater on the team. She was the only debater who grasped the concepts of what we were doing. Add in Williams's hilariously profane speech railing against the judge's use of flowing and they were a formidable team. Flowing is a type of advanced note-taking judges use in debate, but I never learned how to do it. The unfortunate part was no one else won a single round that night.

The next day is where things started to fly off the handle. I met up with Bubo in the hotel lobby and she casually tossed me the keys to one of the vans.

"Doc isn't coming with us today," she said. I asked why and she didn't have a clear answer to the question. I didn't have time to think, so I hopped in the van and followed Bubo and got lost, as usual, since Annapolis could be a tricky place to navigate.

We were almost late for the tournament. I judged the first round at 8:00 a.m. at a Clarion vs. George Mason tilt. I later found out the GMU team went 5–1, with me giving them their lone loss of the prelim rounds. This round illustrated that teams were serious about upholding my wacky judging philosophy, going out of their way to discuss the other team's "racist and sexist language" even when the other team had done nothing wrong. This was an aspect of the philosophy I didn't understand. Even if I didn't see eye to eye with what we were doing before, at least I could go off and judge debates to escape it all. Now thanks to this new judging philosophy, I couldn't even do that.

I judged my first varsity round at Navy, this round being a tilt of Liberty's top team, the married couple Rhett and Samantha Barrett, vs. Wayne State. This round was my first encounter with a stable of debate, the capitalism kritik. Look, I don't think the capitalist system is without flaws. Obviously, unchecked capitalism can lead to nightmare scenarios like October 1929 or September 2008. But what is the alternative? Communism? Socialism? Samantha Barrett was smart enough to throw in a North Korea disadvantage that convinced me not to vote for an end to capitalism as we know it.

Mitch Ball, Liberty's Director of Debate, asked me for the whereabouts of Dr. Bedford, and I didn't quite know what to tell him. For as much as Bedford ranted against Liberty's coaches after the Vanderbilt tournament, Ball seemed legitimately concerned with Doc's well-being.

The overall reaction was more vicious than before. Judges were baffled, and at one point I recall Miriam Bouvier mentioning, "I overheard a group of judges making fun of another judge who voted for Louisville." Keisha Fisher recalled a Boston College debater calling her "an ignorant Black bitch" during a round.

The final tally after the prelim rounds wasn't pretty. Only Josie Jefferson and John Williams went 4–2 and made elims. In this case, making elims felt like being punished. Instead of waking bright and early the next morning and heading out, we had to go back to Navy for an elim round. This was also the day of the NFC and AFC title games, and missing those games was the cherry on top.

I got a peculiar text message from Josie at roughly 2 a.m. The text said be in her room at 8:30 a.m. since a group of debaters were going to confront Dr. Bedford and ask why he didn't show up for the tourney the previous day. I showed up at 8:30, but no one was there. I went back to my room and dozed off, only to be awakened by the sounds of profane shouting coming from Dr. Bedford's room across the hall. I could distinctly hear Miriam and Josie yelling. Dr. Bedford wanted to leave town before the elim round. As Miriam said, "You can get in the van by yourself if you want to, but I'm staying right here—in West Virginia!" A valid point, even though we were in Annapolis.

I recall a conversation with Miriam right before we left for the elim round. Much like Darren, she was horribly discouraged. "I don't even want to be here anymore. I want to quit."

"Nah, don't do that," I replied. "At least go to the final two tournaments, play out the string, and then graduate."

The following year, Miriam Bouvier became the squad's second graduate assistant. At the time, however, Miriam was a single mother increasingly fed up with the dehumanization college debate had wrought. I may not have understood or cared for the current strategy, but I definitely cared about the debaters themselves.

The entire squad wanted nothing to do with Dr. Bedford. He walked alone, while the squad kept a certain distance. His attempt at doing a round circle motivation was met with derision, as his emotionally overwrought, "I may not always be here, but the program will live on!" speech caused John Williams to burst out laughing.

The elim round matched Jefferson and Williams against the aforementioned Liberty couple, the Barretts. The setting was electric, with a full room of debaters and observers. Tom O'Riordan, Navy's Director of Debate, made sure to judge this particular round personally. Josie and John were on their game in this debate, and the Liberty duo somewhat angered me with their condescending attitude toward our strategy. During cross ex, the entire squad repeated the quotes from *The Great Debaters* in unison.

And when the judges' decision came in...we lost 3–0. I can't call it a miscarriage of justice. After all, we weren't even discussing the topic. Some of the judges' comments were intriguing. The other male judge wanted Josie to sing more since he enjoyed her brief burst into song, while the female judge didn't understand what we doing and didn't grasp John's use of rapping. O'Riordan himself was angered by the fact we deliberately went over the nine-minute time limits, even though we requested to have the overtime taken out of prep time.

Dr. Bedford now sprang to life, arguing with O'Riordan in front of the crowd in the room. O'Riordan had already confronted Dr. Bedford about not showing up the previous day, saying, "We lost two rounds that you were supposed to judge, so we're fining you fifteen dollars for each."

"Someone with the squad should have explained my absence," Dr. Bedford replied. He made O'Riordan acknowledge protest as a legit form of debate.

The trip back went only slightly better than the trip there. I rode in Bubo's van, while Dr. Bedford drove another. The weather was rainy instead of snowy. We managed to get lost and wound up in downtown Baltimore, in an area strongly resembling *The Wire*. We ran out of money for the trip, so driving halfway and staying at a hotel was out of the question. We were stuck on the road, and everyone was exhausted. Adding to our road woes, the check engine light came on in Bubo's minivan and we pulled off the road to a gas station. After Miriam recounted the confrontation with Dr. Bedford and his comment of, "This trip has brought out negative things in my life. I ate a candy bar yesterday for the first time in months," I jokingly asked Miriam to go inside and buy me a candy bar, which cracked up the entire group.

While nothing was seriously wrong with the van, we pulled off the road seemingly every thirty minutes for smoke breaks or food. The one highlight of the entire trip occurred when Boyz II Men's "I'll Make Love to You" came on the radio. After hours of hearing incessant marginal 2009–10 era R & B, finally a song everyone knew and cared about. By the time the chorus hit, the entire van sang along, including me. After the song ended, we went back to feeling exhausted. I never understood why Bubo insisted on driving the entire way home rather than having me do some of the driving.

We had taken off from Annapolis at 4 p.m. on Sunday and didn't return to Louisville until 7:30 a.m. on Monday morning. Bubo was practically asleep by the time we reached Bardstown Road and nearly veered into another lane and hit a car. A few minutes later, we arrived back at Davidson Hall.

"Well, we're back in time for our usual 8 a.m. meeting," I quipped. I never felt so exhausted and demoralized in my life. My knees hurt from sitting so long. I wished someone would put me out of my misery. I wished someone would put the debate program out of its misery. I was not happy. No one on the team was happy. The trip to Annapolis had been a total disaster, an even bigger nightmare than usual.

I considered filing a grievance over the insanity that went down on the trip, but decided it wouldn't do any good and would leave me without an assistantship for my second year of grad school. I held my tongue and ranted to my professors about the trip instead, but never filed an official grievance with the administration.

The next few weeks were full of apathy and bewilderment. The team was dissolving before my eyes. Debaters didn't show up. Dr. Bedford wasn't showing up. Marlene, Bubo, and I held down the fort, with the occasional debater popping in. I tried calling and emailing Darren to no avail. Mathers, who is openly gay and discussed it in his speeches, later told me he all but quit the team over an HIV scare and didn't tell anyone but came back to the fold before the next tourney. Carl Vance and Miriam Bouvier were the only team that showed up on a regular basis.

Dr. Bedford had become disconnected from the program. He showed up again after a few weeks and gave a ranting lecture about organizing protesters from Urban Debate Leagues to show up and support us. He also detailed his plan of submitting a series of editorials to major newspapers. He wanted the debaters and staff to read his editorials and make comments. He sent one editorial to the *Washington Post*, criticizing Tom O'Riordan for his role in judging the Liberty debate. To this day, I still don't understand what any of this was supposed to accomplish. Vicky McDonald, baffled as well, noted, "Can we agree the *Washington Post* isn't going to publish this?"

During another of Dr. Bedford's notable rants, he reeled off the names of all the major U of L debaters under his watch and flippantly said, "Oh, and there are whites that go along for the ride with discomfort." I couldn't help but feel this comment was directed at me, which furthered my feelings of marginalization.

On the strategic end of things, the struggling teams would start answering cross ex questions again and drop the *Great Debaters* references. Josie was amused at a comment I made to her in the debate room. "Josie, you are one of my favorite people right now. You took a dilatory partner, a crazy strategy, and somehow went 4–2."

The next tournament was the ADA National Championship back at Vanderbilt, which despite its name is a B-list tournament. This tournament was memorable for the team, and also for me as well, for a couple of reasons. I started to understand how powerful protest debating could be when done right.

The tourney started off nondescriptly. Most of our teams hovered around the .500 mark, aside from Jefferson and Williams, who shockingly ended up going 0–6 for the tourney. They didn't make any adjustments after Navy and used the same exact strategy. Teams had scouted it. McDonald and Abercrombie were improving, toning down the hostile rhetoric toward judges and added in some new Lauryn Hill music that played a key role in explaining the need to rebel. Mathers and Fisher recovered from Navy and went .500 for the tourney.

However, the biggest improvement came from Bouvier and Vance. The tourney was magical considering how nightmarish things had been for them. The duo hit on an argument that resonated with judges in a way few U of L arguments had, namely comparing judges in debate to the Warren Supreme Court in 1954—a group that cast aside their own white privilege in order to make a change and eliminate school segregation. Catching lightning in a bottle, the duo finished 4–2 for the tourney, making the elim rounds. I was proud of them since they had been the only team showing up during that dark February to put in the work.

Vance and Bouvier's elimination round against Liberty was my favorite debate of the year. By now, the duo had gelled with the *Brown vs. Board of Education* argument. This particular Liberty team had run into Josie and John earlier in the tourney and the girl in particular was rattled. The sheer power of Miriam Bouvier's first speech had this girl in tears, which lasted the entire debate as she struggled to ramble through her Habermas evidence. I thought this might be a ploy to carry sympathy with judges, but when she kept this up the entire round, I realized she was sincere. At one point, Carl Vance even called out one of the judges, George Patterson, who I remembered from the first trip to Nashville when he judged the McDonald/Abercrombie debate against Emory.

Despite his ultra-traditional philosophy, I knew Patterson was an okay guy since he saw the exact same debate as me back in October. And sure enough, Patterson was the deciding vote as Bouvier and Vance won 2–1. I'm still not entirely sure what the one judge saw when he voted for Liberty. To me, if you make the other team cry and break their will, you win the debate. As Patterson said to me after the round, "I almost voted for you last time. You just have to give me something."

That night we celebrated with a team meal at Olive Garden, which was memorable for an amusing misunderstanding with the waitress. She asked us who we were, to which Dr. Bedford replied, "We're the University of Louisville debate team, in town for the ADA nationals. We have a duo in the Elite 8 now." The waitress pointed at Carl and me before Miriam promptly corrected her. Carl Vance and I were the only two white people at the table. I can't understand why she thought I was a debater since I was thirty years old and starting to have a hint of gray around the temples. For the first time I felt abuzz about the team's potential, barely sleeping that night from thinking about the win over Liberty.

If the Liberty round proved triumphant, the Elite 8 round against Vanderbilt's #1 seeded team of Carter Morris and Noah Braun was a low point, from ecstasy to agony in a matter of hours. Morris won an honorary award the night before, which our team planned to use as offense against him. In addition, we planned to use some Vandy novice debaters' comments against them as well, in which one asked Darren Mathers, "You all are so stupid, do you ever win?"

Morris and Braun might not have been the greatest team in college debate, but they were the best I saw in terms of dealing with our protest. They forced their topical discussion on us, insisting they were a protest as well, an on-topic protest against enriched uranium and nuclear destruction. The debate turned petty and embarrassing when Bouvier/Vance launched personal attacks against Morris for winning his award and the whole plan backfired. This one was a definite 3–0 loss, and Morris/Braun went on to win the ADA championship. Thus began a rivalry with Vanderbilt that lasted the rest of my time with the program.

Regardless of the Vandy outcome, there was at least some light at the end of the tunnel. We had one tournament left on the schedule, and it was the big one, the Cross Examination Debate Association national tourney, taking place at Cal Berkeley. There was also the National Debate Tournament as well, but no one on our squad qualified for it. CEDA is open to everyone, while the NDT is restricted to the absolute top teams in the country. During the buildup for CEDA, rumors started making the rounds that the administration might be planning to cut the program's budget. To prevent this, the squad needed to make a strong showing at CEDA.

Dr. Bedford entered Bubo and himself in the Pro Debaters tourney, a charity event held the day before CEDA. He practiced his speech in the debate room before we left, and it was quite the speech. He went off on a tirade about white privileged forms of competition and made the metaphor that debate was a "white cave bitch" oppressing the "Black hoes" of Louisville but was all too enticing for a Black male debater like himself. It was a surreal and offensive speech that shocked everyone on the team, Marlene Mayhew in particular, who curled up in a ball on the couch in the back of the room.

Dr. Bedford's speech provided some amusing moments in the following days. Darren ran some of his new speech by me, where he planned to quote Maya Angelou's *I Know Why the Caged Bird Sings*. I jokingly responded, "Yeah, that's good, Darren, but guess what? I know why the cave bitch sings." Darren almost fell to the floor with laughter. What else was there to do but have some fun?

Shockingly enough, Dr. Bedford and Bubo won the Pro Debaters tournament despite the fact Bubo refused to compete and sat in the audience. Dr. Bedford spun her refusal to compete as her being invisible, and the debate community needed to change in order to make her visible. While he edited out the "cave bitch" and "Black ho" references, the speech was still wild stuff, and the other coaches debating in this tourney purely for fun were stunned. Bubo's refusal to compete with Dr. Bedford was the first hint to me that something was wrong between them.

After the pro tournament, Dr. Bedford half-jokingly mentioned, "Maybe next year I should team with Brian for the Pro Debaters tourney!"

"Do I get to sit in the crowd and be invisible?" I asked.

"That argument might take some work!" he laughed, oblivious to the notion I had become more or less invisible within the team.

CEDA was a wild experience. For the first time, I witnessed novices, JV teams, and varsity teams all competing in the same tourney. Before the rounds started, Dr. Bedford gave us a speech saying, "You all have it in you to win this thing. You should not drop a single ballot, just like we didn't drop a single ballot yesterday in the pro tourney!" Say what you will about his methods, but the man could certainly give a hype speech before a tourney.

For once, everyone had fun debating. Even the usually serious Natalie Abercrombie finished in the top twenty speakers for the tourney. Abercrombie was a terrific public speaker but had no experience in debate. Vicky McDonald was the experienced debater of the two and had paid her dues, so I was happy to see them go 5–3 and make elims. Whether due to more favorable judging or facing a pool also including novices and JV teams, or our own improvement, everyone made elims at 5–3, including novices Mathers and Fisher.

One elim round reinforced my perception of judging as being a political act. Bouvier/Vance stomped the Cornell team they faced in the opening elim round, yet only won 2–1 because judge Gretchen Stedman steadfastly refused to ever vote for a Louisville team. She obviously hated our strategy, but some of her disdain stemmed from a personal vendetta dating back to 2004 when her Michigan State team lost a round to Louisville and a U of L debater told her to "Keep it gangsta, Gretchen."

Every one of U of L's duos lost in the exact same elimination round, which was quite eerie and had the feeling of glass-ceiling collusion. "Give them a few wins to shut them up, but for God's sake, don't let them go too far." Mathers and Fisher decided to compete in a novice breakout bracket against Folsom Lake College rather than the main elims. I didn't see this particular round, since Darren and Keisha felt me filming them would make them nervous, so I watched Towson's elim round against USC instead.

Towson was a trip to watch. Essentially Towson was a more militant kindred spirit of Louisville's in the debate community. Deven Cooper originally debated for U of L before having a falling-out with Dr. Bedford, so he transferred to Towson and ran an improved version of the Bedford strategy. In 2008, Cooper and his partner, Dayvon Love, won the CEDA championship, with a runner-up finish in 2009.

Towson's round vs. USC was jam-packed with onlookers highly entertained by Towson's Black militant style of performance debate. After the decision was announced as a 3–0 for Towson, I joked to Dayvon in the hallway, "You guys are such assholes. We talk about 'Make us visible, please!' while you guys say, 'We are visible and we're here to beat your ass.'" Love laughed out loud at my assessment.

I wondered what our novices were doing, however. As I walked down the hall, I heard more and more commotion, and then talked to Darren, Bubo, and Dr. Bedford. The round hadn't gone well. We had lost a 2–1 decision to a couple of "really horrible" girls from Folsom

Lake due to a judge who viciously attacked our strategy and accused the novices of being incapable of writing such speeches (which they had).

"He told us the minute we said 'protest' he decided against us. But, man, I could tell from how bad those girls sucked that we were back in novice," Darren said. Indeed, this judge even confronted Dr. Bedford and Bubo in the hallway and had an argument so heated both of them had to walk away. All in all, an unpleasant way to end what had been an exciting tournament.

We spent the next day watching Towson debate as the elims went on. Dev Murray and Adam Jackson were an excellent team, but alas they would fall to Whitman College, who ran six different arguments against them and won a 2–1 decision. I spent most of Sunday in a drunken Heineken-induced haze, watching elim debates and some of the NCAA Elite 8 games. We were in Oakland, after all. The city has two things going against it: there's nothing to do, and it is also a scary and dangerous place. I couldn't even find a decent sports bar to watch WrestleMania.

I was the only Louisville staff member who bothered to attend the finals of the tourney. Whitman faced off against defending champion Oklahoma, who had unseated Towson the previous year. After all of our protesting of the CEDA bylaws, speed, and white privileged competition, I watched the debate and saw four white guys spew down at 400 words per minute. I don't remember anything said, since I was still drunk. I couldn't help but wonder why anyone sober would want to watch this debate. Sitting behind me were Carter Morris and Noah Braun from Vanderbilt, who I congratulated on their win over U of L at the ADA while the judges tallied up their flow notes.

"Hey, I want to apologize to you guys for what we did back at the ADAs," I said. "Going after you personally was not a good idea and sounded better in the van on the way to the building. Your nuclear protest strategy was the best stuff anyone has run on us."

"Nah, it's cool," Morris replied. "We really enjoy debating you all."

Soon after, the nine judges announced their decision. Oklahoma won 6-3 to repeat as champions.

Upon returning to Louisville, Dr. Bedford thanked me for everything I'd done for the team as we walked past the shops at Standiford Field. The next week would involve putting together the various videos filmed at CEDA for future use in the debate room. I was ready to finish the semester on a high note.

I saw little of the debaters once we returned from Oakland. I spent most of the next month in the debate room talking with Marlene about the future direction of the program. At one point, I asked her what I could do to feel more welcome by everyone on the team.

"I think the problem others on the team have with you is this: you have never once confronted your own white privilege and as a result they don't know what to think of you," Marlene said. "The debaters on the team are from a different age group and ethnicity than you, so it is hard for them to relate to you, and vice versa."

I have thought about that moment long and hard, but I must say what she suggested is easier said than done. I was only then becoming aware of these concepts and how I have benefited. At the time all I could do was fire back at her, "Do you realize I went to high school at Butler in the 1990s? That place was a retro 1950s school reeking of whiteness. I need years to undo that brainwashing."

In the end, I wonder if I helped aid in my own exclusion from the team. Perhaps I let my own frustration at our strategy changes bother me and it led to being excluded in other areas such as personal friendships. The season itself ended up being surprisingly decent, despite the chaotic scenarios outlined throughout.

The University of Louisville debate team had in fact been marginalized by the debate community, and ironically enough, I felt marginalized to some extent and rendered invisible by the team. I recall a judge from Oklahoma's words as he critiqued one of Josie and John's rounds at CEDA: "Sometimes I feel like you render yourselves invisible." I can relate. I do think U of L succeeded to a degree in becoming visible again in the debate community.

The 2009–10 school year was an emotionally draining experience to say the least. I went from feeling utter puzzlement, to frustration, to outright despair, and then finally feeling relatively upbeat about the way things turned out. Regardless of feeling at times like being involved with the Malcom X Debate Team would be the end of me, I was ready to come back for another year. Major changes were in store for the U of L debate program during the 2010–11 school year, some of which are still being felt today.

CHAPTER 10

ANARCHY IN THE U OF L

I eagerly returned to the Malcom X Debate Team at U of L for the 2010–11 school year. My first year of grad school had been an up-and-down experience. I certainly hoped the second year with the debate program would be smoother, with less drama and overall chaos. I was about as wrong as anyone possibly could be. The 2010–11 U of L debate team isn't by any means considered legendary in the realm of college debate, but given what we went through, maybe it should be.

The August retreat was less bizarre than the prior year, where we spent a copious amount of time reading Dr. Kendall Bedford's blog entries about his July 2009 arrest. There were several returning debaters from the previous year's team: Darren Mathers and Keisha Fisher, Vicky McDonald and Natalie Abercrombie, and the newly formed team of Carl Vance and John Williams. Both of those guys needed a new partner since Josie Jefferson graduated and Miriam Bouvier was now the team's other graduate assistant. Josie stayed on as an unofficial coach. Darren and Keisha moved up from novice to varsity.

There was new talent for the novice ranks. Sandra Morton and Amber Burns were the latest Black female recruits, while the other two recruits were two white guys named Doug Lusco and Preston Bates. I immediately took to Amber since she was a fellow Butler alum, albeit graduating a decade later. I never found out much about Sandra's background since we never clicked on a personal level. Doug was a high school debater from the Northern Kentucky/Cincinnati area (by way of New York) who took an interest in U of L's racially-based strategies despite being one of whitest dudes you'll ever meet.

Preston was the wild card of this group, an ultra-privileged sort from Prospect by way of Austin, Texas. There couldn't have been a more inappropriate member for this incarnation of U of L debate, and I don't believe he had Doug's high school debating background. Preston was a die-hard libertarian, which he trumpeted quite often in the debate room, in the car on the way to tournaments, and everywhere else outside of the actual debates. He irritated some on the team when he marked "Other" on his application in the race/ethnicity category, claiming to be some part Native American. He was similar to some of our opponents in that regard, distancing himself from whiteness. Most of the other debaters never knew what to make of Preston. He was smoother than Kyle Resnick, another white male recruit who quickly wore out his welcome. Only Marlene Mayhew and I understood Preston and his political leanings. Marlene was repulsed by Preston. I was amused by him.

As far as my own role with the team, Dr. Bedford and I agreed that I would film and edit a documentary about the team's 2010–11 season. I planned to use this as my practicum project for my Communication MA program, and if it was well made, we could do something more with it. I often messed around with the team's camera for this project, a fact which angered Marlene during one day of the retreat. I was busy filming people in the debate room instead of helping her heave various food dishes. Marlene dropped the heavy container, and a fire briefly broke out in the room. So far, my hopes for a smoother year hadn't come to pass.

The novices had to do some of the same speeches I performed the previous year, but thankfully this stuff was cut down to simple "Tell us about yourself" speeches. The main activity of the retreat involved a field trip to the National Underground Railroad Freedom Center in Cincinnati. On the way there, Dr. Bedford amused the newbies by singing along to his *Prince's Greatest Hits* CD, while I wished he had put on the Toni Braxton CD instead. Preston also annoyed Marlene, who usually ran the office but came with us on this trip, by discussing some rather questionable and sexist moments from *American Psycho*.

This was my first trip to Cincinnati, despite living ninety minutes away my entire life. The museum itself was about what one would expect, with lots of displays of slave quarters from the 1800s, quotes from various presidents on slavery, and displays of the Underground Railroad–era Cincinnati. The squad was interested, but Dr. Bedford seemed profoundly moved. I've never seen anyone else who wore his heart on his sleeve quite as much as him. He was on the verge of tears for most of the tour.

The next day, we discussed what we saw at the museum and how it might relate to the CEDA resolution. For the record, the resolution for 2010–11 was the following:

"The United States Federal Government should substantially increase the number of and/or substantially expand beneficiary eligibility for its visas for one or more of the following: employment-based immigrant visas, nonimmigrant temporary worker visas, family-based visas, human trafficking–based visas."

Dr. Bedford, still emotional over the experience, led off the discussion. "I have to say, that trip was powerful yesterday. In fact, I think what we should do is base our entire strategy off of the trip to the Underground Museum."

I was baffled as to what he meant, and as events would unfold, this idea never came to pass anyway. The conversation turned to me and my role in whatever this Underground Railroad of Debate strategy might be.

"I found it interesting that in the presidential quotes section, every president up until Lincoln all decried slavery as an awful institution, yet nearly all of them owned slaves," I said.

"Brian, I think you are somewhat like Reverend Rankin, who

guided runaway slaves to freedom in the North," Dr. Bedford replied. "In this case, you can guide these young white men, Doug and Preston, into the realm of what we do here in this program."

"I don't know if I feel comfortable with that analogy," I replied.

"Because you feel it cheapens what Rankin did?" Marlene inquired.

"Well, yeah. But if you want me to help mentor these guys, I will gladly do so."

All of this discussion was sound and fury signifying nothing. School started back the next week, but Dr. Bedford didn't last much longer with the debate team. By early September, something was obviously wrong with Doc. He seemed increasingly erratic in the debate room, and even stranger than usual.

The final blowup occurred when the team prepared for Georgia State, our first tourney of the year. I was sitting at my computer not far from Marlene's desk, both partitioned off from the rest of the debate room via bookshelves. Doc and Bubo conversed by her cubicle, and all of a sudden, his temper started flaring. I stood up to watch the epic meltdown he directed at Bubo.

"Don't you know how much I love you? Don't you know how much I've sacrificed? Well, I've had enough. Figure it out for yourselves. Fuck all of you. I'm gone!" He stormed out, slamming the door behind him, never to be seen in the debate room again. I felt physically ill having to hear that tirade. My stomach was in knots for the next hour. Bubo, as usual, took things in stride.

I already knew some of what was wrong with him. Back in May 2010, Marlene and I were the only ones coming to the debate room as the semester was winding down. I stopped by one final time before the semester officially ended to say bye, and then we started talking. Marlene revealed some things that had baffled me since January.

"You do know why Dr. Bedford didn't show up that one day at Navy, right?"

"No, I have no idea. I thought it was some bizarre attempt at motivation, an act of mad genius I didn't grasp," I said.

"Doc has had this unrequited love for Brittany Pollard for a long time now, even though both of them have been married. Well, I guess he's about to be divorced, but she's still married. Anyway, when the team went to Annapolis, she met up with an old friend of hers who lives in D.C. Doc was so insanely jealous he threw a fit and refused to go to the tournament."

"Are you serious? I met this friend of hers in the lobby for about ten seconds and he wished us luck. There was nothing inappropriate going on that I noticed. And here I thought Dr. Bedford was some mad genius. He was a lovesick fool all along."

The situation with Dr. Kendall Bedford and the U of L administration got worse as the semester went on. While he never came back to Davidson 101, the specter of him hung over the team like a dark cloud. He became the subject of a full investigation for sexual harassment, with rumors of emails he had sent to Bubo. He countered with his own complaints against her and the administration in general, and the exact details of his departure are still hazy. By the end of 2011, the founder of the Malcom X Debate Team was no longer employed by the University of Louisville.

With or without Doc, we still had a tourney to prepare for at Georgia State in Atlanta. Miriam started doing more hands-on coaching with the novices, while Bubo dealt with the varsity teams. I filmed practice speeches while also posting evidence and judging philosophies on the Tabroom website. Tabroom was curious to me. It's a website where all the teams in a particular tourney post their sources and evidence, while judges post their philosophies of what they want to see in a debate. I understood the judges' part, but teams posting all their evidence seemed akin to an NFL team posting their playbook on NFL.com for the world to see. I posted a few things, but not a huge amount since everyone already knew what we were doing. Bubo worked on judge preferences, which is another oddity of debate. Teams list which judges they prefer, and rounds are created with mutually agreed upon judges in mind. That was why hardcore policy teams faced each other, while teams such as U of L and Towson often met.

The varsity strategy echoed what we ended with the previous year, aside from the discussion of various debate norms. Bubo decided to cut the criticisms of speed and judging flows. None of it contributed to very many wins, but what were we doing instead? Whiteness. Tons of blocks about whiteness, white privilege, and white supremacy. A nonstop barrage of Tim Wise, bell hooks, Audre Lorde, David Hall, Peggy McIntosh, and anyone else who wrote about the subject. The idea consisted of using these scholars to set a framework of who could do the best job of deconstructing whiteness in society (or debate itself). We still eschewed any topical discussion, which I found odd since immigration reform was clearly a topic that fed into racial arguments.

Bubo also put the kibosh on my documentary project, noting I would need countless release forms to even attempt such a thing, which wasn't feasible. I agreed and instead dedicated myself to writing a practicum paper on the previous year's debate team (the bulk of which formed the basis of the prior two chapters).

Since the novices weren't remotely ready, they stayed home for the first tourney in Atlanta. Thankfully, the tourney itself took place over a weekend in mid-September, so we avoided the horrible Atlanta traffic. Atlanta was a nice city outside of rush hour. It seemed like a booming metro area, the buildings were stunning from the downtown view at GSU, and the city had money for infrastructure and interstates.

Truth be told, our varsity teams never clicked the entire year. These problems would manifest themselves more as the school year went on, but I felt a decided hangdog air about the squad's performance at Georgia State. No one posted awful 0–6 records like the previous year when we did the flat-out protest debates, but no one was standing out either. We had a bunch of duos hovering around .500 and missing the elims.

The most notable debate of the tourney for me personally wasn't one of our debates, but instead one I judged between Towson's team of Enrique Burns and Denny Brogan vs. UT San Antonio. I was assigned this debate because Miriam and Enrique were a romantic item, having met at CEDA back in March. As such, Miriam was disqualified from judging Towson debates, and I got the assignment. This debate turned highly personal and made me extremely uncomfortable judging it, since these white UTSA guys had a grudge with Towson over a loss at CEDA. That round boiled down to Towson goading one of these guys into admitting he was bisexual, and now they ranted about visible identities vs. invisible identities. Burns and Brogan employed a strategy I hadn't seen before which blew my mind: Quare theory. Quare is an intersectionality argument of Black and gay and made for quite a potent debate strategy.

I voted for Towson but felt dirty about doing so. In my decision I praised and chastised both teams. "The dilemma you guys had (UTSA) is the whole invisible identity thing you discussed here can be just that, invisible. As far as you guys go (Towson), I have some reservations about what you are doing here. I know why I am here, and I'm pretty sure quare doesn't apply to one of you, so I wonder how this debate would have gone if UTSA had asked if you are really ethical advocates for quare." The UTSA guys had debated until they were red in the face but boxed themselves in with their own strategy. I don't think Burns and Brogan were happy with the win.

During lunch, I made sure to discuss this round with our team, especially Darren. "I judged a Towson debate where Enrique Burns and Denny Brogan ran this quare argument. It was new to me."

"Wait, they were doing *what*?" Carl Vance asked. "Miriam, I think you need to have a talk with Enrique about them doing that."

"Darren, have you ever heard of quare?" I asked. "It's something you should consider for the future. It fits you perfectly."

"I haven't heard of it, but I will check it out when we get back," Darren replied.

On our team, I already knew about Darren since he was open about his sexuality. What I didn't know was Carl and John were also gay, which I have to admit surprised me. Marlene was a divorced mother of two but had become a lesbian as she had entered her 40s, feeling the time was right to recognize her true self.

On the trip home, the team had a conversation about our direction going forward, especially the novices. "What was Doc possibly thinking? Bringing in two other white male debaters?" Miriam ranted.

"At least he didn't bring in some white girls," Keisha replied. "I can deal with the white boys easier than I can white girls."

I said nothing at the time, but looking back I understood the method to the madness in this case. I thought Dr. Bedford brought both Preston and Doug in to give me someone to bond with, since I was so isolated the prior year. Strategically, they could also prove amusing, using two ultra white guys as a weapon against whiteness. The previous year I noticed much of the vitriol from opponents and judges happened when I wasn't around.

I felt increasingly frustrated with the varsity teams. There were fundamental problems beyond the strategy. Some, like Natalie, seemed more and more beaten down by it all. Often times, Miriam took the novices off to another room to work with them, which was a shame since what they were doing interested me more than the varsity teams. Doug and Amber were paired together, with Preston and Sandra being the other novice team.

The next tourney was held at West Georgia in Carrollton, about an hour west of Atlanta. I was back to driving to a tourney, with Preston and Doug in tow. Bubo put us white guys together in a Hyundai Elantra, while everyone else rode in vans. Preston always sat in the passenger seat, with Doug in the back seat. I could sense Doug was having trouble with our strategy, while Preston more or less took it in stride. Doug was quite sincere about debate, while Preston looked at it as the sort of roleplaying U of L usually dismissed.

"So, I hear the novices are doing some topical evidence in addition to the whiteness?" I asked.

"Yeah, we are also advocating for increasing visas for immigrants," Doug revealed. "What I can't deal with is this whole idea of making moral arguments. You can't do that in debate."

"Should we make immoral arguments then, Doug?" I pondered.

"Well, that isn't what I mean. In debate, it's supposed to be all about your plan, a topical plan. You don't discuss issues like abortion because it's a moral stance. Say what you want about Towson's whole Black Rage/Kill Whitey argument, but it's an actual *plan*. My high school debate coach warned me about this. He told me to debate the Louisville strategy you need to already be a master of debate, which is funny since it's supposed to be something a novice can pick up quickly."

"I've been working on my speech. Do you want to hear it?" Preston asked. I nodded and he read his zany speech, which discussed increasing immigration to combat the armies of whiteness. It wasn't half bad for a beginner. Once he finished, the topic turned back to the state of the team itself.

"I am worried about the future of this program," Preston said. "Without Dr. Bedford around, we don't have a tenured faculty member leading this team, and I really don't see how the administration will let things continue this way."

"I don't know. I'm out of here after this year anyway, but I understand your concerns," I replied.

"Yeah, you'll have a master's in communication, not a serious major," Preston retorted, oblivious to how I might take offense. I tried to stay focused on debate matters.

"I'm glad you all are going to be somewhat on topic, though. Last year I felt Darren and Keisha became dehumanized due to our strategy. Don't let them dehumanize you at these tournaments. You have to argue with these people. That's the biggest problem I have always had with what we do, the lack of engaging our opponents. Believe me, most of these people are educated idiots. If you listen to the stupid shit they spew, they'll give you everything you'll need to beat them. Our strategy is a house of cards as presently constructed, but it doesn't have to be if you engage the opponent."

"We should do more class-based arguments. Or I wish we would do more of a protest," Preston replied.

"Trust me. You don't want to do the pure protest," I said wearily.

The trip to West Georgia provided some laughs. During a brief food stop in Dalton, GA, I pulled the rented Hyundai up by Bubo's rented minivan and put the window down. Preston, Doug, and I all riffed on Justin Bieber's "Baby" with our own version.

"Whiteness, whiteness, whiteness, ooooh! It's just whiteness, whiteness, whiteness, noooo!" Bubo laughed out loud at our rendition, then started singing the real version herself.

After a brief detour driving on the wrong road, we finally found the University of West Georgia. Marlene and Bubo always insisted on printed out directions instead of using a GPS, and as a result we got lost constantly. If the Georgia State tourney left me feeling blasé, the West Georgia tourney actively pissed me off and embarrassed me.

Bubo gave the team some final advice before the tourney started, noting the importance of debating ethically and the importance of building coalitions before the usual "Black Power!" chant. An attractive Asian girl walked by, and Preston took notice of her. Preston turned to me and jested, "I'm here to build coalitions—with my cock." Preston professed to having a fascination with "ethnic girls."

One of the main debates I observed and filmed was Darren and Keisha vs. a Georgia Tech team consisting of an East Indian guy and a white guy. Darren played some Lil Wayne stuff from his rap/metal album, the exact purpose of which eluded me. The debate itself was a typical capitalism debate, with the East Indian guy whining about capitalism harming him, we countered with whiteness, then they ran a permutation saying, "We can fight both our capitalist and white oppressors!"

Keisha's final speech was a complete fiasco. "They are talking about capitalism but fuck all that shit. They don't know what the fuck they are talking about, and I don't care!" She went on this way for six solid minutes. My face was in my hands by the end of this meltdown. Before the judge's decision, I pulled the team into the hallway.

"So how do you think we did?" Darren asked excitedly.

"Darren, I don't think you all won that one."

Judge Hank Avera came back with his decision. He gave the Georgia guys the ballot on their permutation, but in his amusing hippie way tried to make both teams feel good. "This debate was beautiful, man. It gave me a lot to think about. I enjoyed the Lil Wayne song. I know my music. But at the end of the day, Louisville doesn't really have an answer as to why we can't fight both capitalism and whiteness." The Indian guy asked me if I would send him a link to the YouTube clip of the debate when I posted it. I never did. Bubo didn't want that debate to see the light of day.

The most notable debate I judged was between Vanderbilt's top novices, who always wore suits, and a lone African girl from West Georgia, whose partner no showed the tourney. This was where I first heard the strategy that would become the bane of U of L's existence: Speciesism. Vanderbilt's plan insisted the United States should expand the definition of citizenship to include all sentient beings. This poor girl from West Georgia was overwhelmed and angered, since for all intents and purposes, Vanderbilt was comparing her African immigrant status to farm animals. I gave Vandy the ballot but felt dirty, since the West Georgia girl was debating alone and had no strategy against speciesism. I felt the need to discuss the outcome with the Vanderbilt team.

"So, did you enjoy lunch? I had a burrito."

"Yeah, it was fine. We had burritos too," one of them replied.

"Speciesism!" I exclaimed. Even their coach, Cindy Bader, a voluptuous blonde woman in her 20s, laughed. I later learned Carl Vance and John Williams ran into another Vanderbilt team that ran speciesism against them, but John asked the exact same question about lunch.

"After that, they kicked the speciesism," John said.

Results wise, the tournament hadn't gone much better for the varsity teams. Everyone was .500 or worse, with most of these losses either being because the other team ran topicality with us on the affirmative or used a permutation when we were on the negative. Preston and Sandra performed well for their first tourney but lost in an elim to Vanderbilt. Doug and Amber also did quite well, getting all the way to the semis and thus keeping us at this place longer than we needed to be. This was always a problem with making elims. We usually lost, and thus never could take off on the long trip back home until after 4:00.

Doug and Amber of course lost to the Vanderbilt speciesism pricks in a 3–0 decision. The debate was frustrating since this whole absurd speciesism argument had so many holes in it. I don't think it ever worked much for their team at the varsity level, but it could wreak havoc on inexperienced novices. As I would find out, they ran it against teams who used racially-oriented arguments, like some form of twisted satire.

On the way home, Doug and I vowed to stop speciesism at all costs. Preston, for his part, felt torn on the subject. "I honestly see where they are coming from with speciesism. As a dog owner, I even kind of agree with them. But then as a libertarian, I also don't want the government to decide that sort of thing. I would side with racist business owners who didn't want to serve Black people. Let the free market decide and they will go out of business without the government interfering."

"Preston, why did you join this debate team again?" I asked.

"The scholarship money," he replied.

"Look, my paternal grandfather was one step away from being a Klansman with his racism," I mentioned. "He ran a segregated diner and gas station near Miami back in the early '60s. He did quite well financially by only serving whites in the area. What caused him to close up shop was a combination of protestors and federal law. He moved to rural North Carolina rather than change."

Preston had no response.

A few days later I looked into the issue of speciesism and the criticisms of it. I typically didn't do a ton of evidence research, leaving it to the debaters themselves. I was taking three grad-level classes and didn't have to conduct research for them, but in this case, I made an exception. Evidence wasn't hard to find. I checked the Wikipedia entry on speciesism, back sourced what I needed, and printed out a section from Peter Staudenmaier criticizing speciesism as an offensive analogy to the Civil Rights Movement, something promoted by fringe animal rights groups. This took about thirty seconds. I handed copies to Preston and Doug, figuring Amber and Sandra wouldn't care.

The next debate meeting featured an autopsy on what had gone wrong at West Georgia. Bubo posed the question of what we needed to do to win. Similar to the prior year, I decided to chime in.

"I saw several of our debates at West Georgia," I said. "Right now, we have two major problems. One is people running topicality on us. The other is permutations. As long as we are off topic, judges may give the other team the topicality argument, so I don't know what to do about that. As far as perms go, we have to do something to explain why they can't. We keep saying 'You can't perm a protest,' but that doesn't mean judges aren't allowing it."

Bubo agreed with me in part. While the varsity teams never tried anything topical, she told the various varsity debaters we needed evidence explaining why someone can't perm our strategy. Also frustrating was that so many teams ran the strategy "They aren't on topic and thus are a moving target and not predictable." If nothing else, we were constantly predictable. The overall strategy remained a work in progress. The team had one last tournament in the Fall 2010 semester at Wake Forest.

CHAPTER 11

DEBATE WILL BE THE END OF ME

The Frank R. Shirley Classic at Wake Forest was a major tourney, one which we skipped the previous year due to scrapping our initial strategy. A few days before the tourney, I mentioned to Preston something I would live to regret.

"These tournaments are really draining, so I am considering bringing some beer to unwind at night," I said. "If you want, bring a six pack of your own. I don't think anyone cares. Hell, half of CEDA was trashed out of their minds last year." Preston was 22 and thus of legal drinking age, so I didn't think my comment was a big deal. Sure enough, when the time came, I brought some Sam Adams and Preston brought something of his own.

Upon arriving at Davidson Hall early that November morning, we found out a bombshell: Natalie Abercrombie had quit the team. I hadn't seen many of her debates with Vicky in the first two tourneys but noticed at squad meetings she was more and more withdrawn. Natalie was the sort that sat quietly and brooded. She wasn't overtly angry, but instead let what opponents said hurt her deeply inside. Still, Natalie quitting threw Vicky for a loop, since now she had no partner and acted as an assistant coach for the Wake Forest tourney. I took tried to lighten her mood by going up to her and whispering "Whiteness..." in silly fashion.

"It encompasses everything," she replied with a wink.

I drove another crappy rented Hyundai Elantra from Enterprise, with Preston and Doug riding with me. Once we took off from U of L, Preston remarked, "Thank God I'm in this car where I can go back to being my asshole whiteness self." I shook my head, while Doug chuckled. I realized Doug was starting to look up to Preston, which gave me pause. Preston was a smooth-talking cat, and for a while I think even Bubo looked the other way at his absences from squad meetings.

The trip to Winston-Salem went through West Virginia. After the Annapolis trip in January, I wasn't looking forward to it. The weather was better, but the car itself was not. As we stopped in Bluefield, West Virginia, I noticed the steering wheel had a certain jittery feel to it, the same sort of feeling my old Oldsmobile had when the tires needed to be replaced. We stopped at a Starbucks for a few minutes, but I worried about driving the car as we left.

Back on the road, we went through a tunnel and crossed into Virginia. I drove almost eighty to keep up with Bubo and Miriam. We were a few miles outside Bland, Virginia, when suddenly a terrifying explosion shocked us. The left front tire had burst, and we went careening toward the median on I-77. I slammed the brakes as hard as possible to avoid a serious wreck, then managed to stop the car on the left side of the road. We took a minute to collect ourselves after this brush with death. Soon after, I called Bubo.

"Hey, we just had a flat tire. I'm about to call AAA, but I don't feel great about driving this car all the way to Winston-Salem on a spare tire. Can we exchange the car at the next town with an Enterprise?"

"Yes. For now, stay put and wait for AAA," Bubo said with eerie calm. "We will be waiting for you in Wytheville. That's the nearest Enterprise."

After I called AAA, we waited for a tow truck to arrive. Preston wanted to change the tire, but I advised against doing so. Soon after, a Virginia state trooper pulled up in back of us and approached the car.

"I see you boys had a flat. You're on the wrong side of the road. Let me block off traffic while you slowly move to the right side to wait for the tow truck."

That went surprisingly well. The trooper blocked off enough traffic so I could start the car and muster enough momentum to reach the other side of the road on three tires. We thanked him for his help, and he moved on. This might sound sad, but on such an occasion I was glad to be in the car with two other white guys and not with the rest of the team. Would there have been an incident with the state trooper if the mostly Black group had a flat? I would hope not, but it was a moment that made me ponder if we had any sort of white privilege in this case. Soon after, the AAA guy arrived, put on the spare, and we went on our merry way to the Enterprise in Wytheville.

"I'm glad the cop didn't check our luggage in the trunk," Preston said. "I have some weed in there with the beer."

"You have *what*?!" I yelled.

After this arduous ordeal, we arrived at the University Inn, not far from Wake Forest, right in time for the opening tournament ceremony. The punchline for the entire day was after risking life and limb to reach Winston-Salem, we were rewarded with having to listen to UK's debate coach give a speech.

I saw little of the novices at Wake Forest since the novice rounds were held ninety minutes away at Appalachian State. I wanted to see if they were running the Staudenmaier evidence in the event they ran into Vanderbilt. Preston was now drawing a full x/y intercept chart on the board to illustrate immigration and whiteness. I was stuck judging debates or watching our varsity teams. During lunch, Bubo, Vicky, and I had a conversation about something that needed to be discussed. Keisha Fisher was becoming a problem.

"Keisha hasn't adapted to varsity very well. Right now, I almost think she is holding Darren down," Bubo said.

"She flies off the handle at the first sign of anything wrong in a debate," Vicky interjected.

"Keisha's stuff is so me, me, me in the debates," I said. "If we are railing against white privilege, she undermines the basic strategy since she clearly is someone that comes from a privileged background herself." For the time being, we left Keisha alone to debate the way she wanted..

The last debate of Day One was a highlight of the tourney, matching Darren and Keisha against Enrique and Denny from Towson. I wasn't judging so I made sure to watch this one, as did Vicky. Deven Cooper coached the Towson team. The debate itself was hilarious, as Enrique unleashed this ultra militant speech about how "we are going to take power, by force if we need to. By any means necessary!" He also ranted about the downfall of the Black Panthers and how so many are "dead or in jail." Once the debate went to prep time, I rushed over to Vicky and Deven.

"Are you watching this?" I whispered to them, semi-laughing.

"This debate has had some problems," chuckled Deven. He had the "dead or in jail" comment scribbled and underlined on a sheet of paper.

During the rebuttals, I kept begging for our team to call out Towson's militant lunacy and position us as a saner alternative. Come on, Darren. They gave us what we needed to beat them. In his last speech, Darren got to the point.

"They have said all of these things about violence, but that isn't a solution. Their own evidence noted the Black Panthers ended up dead or in jail. We are about changing the world in a more peaceful way," Darren proclaimed. That was all we needed. The judge, a white male in this case, was all too glad to give us the ballot.

After the debates, the novices, Vicky, and me ate at the diner next to the hotel. This was a fun bit of relaxation after a stressful couple of days, as we talked about various romantic relationships, team gossip, and anything else. Amber looked at Preston, Doug, and me and said, "We were so terrified after you had the flat tire. We thought you were dead."

On this trip, Darren stayed in the same room as Preston, Doug, and me. We celebrated a solid day of debating by downing all the beer.

Technically, Darren and Doug were slightly underage, but I figured if you could join the army at nineteen or twenty, you should be able to drink a beer. Our novice teams were winning, with the varsity teams treading water yet again, but the win over Towson felt important. I tried to go to sleep, but the other guys snuck out to go to the nearby liquor store. Preston went on another beer run, this time for Yuengling, which was exotic and unavailable at that time in Kentucky.

They woke me up when they returned, and I couldn't go back to sleep. Instead, I asked for another beer, and we had an impromptu discussion of anything we could think of at the time. Darren was oddly downbeat, despite the Towson win.

"I don't know. I'm still stunned by this Natalie thing. I can't believe she quit. Doc and Bubo thought she was the heir apparent. If she couldn't handle the pressure, what chance do any of us have?" Darren pondered, sipping his Yuengling.

"Darren, let me tell you something," I said. "You are ten times the debater Natalie Abercrombie ever was. I don't care if she finished Top 20 in speaker points at CEDA. That's all she could do, a nice, sassy Black girl speech. I have watched Vicky McDonald and her debate, and Vicky had to hold her hand through every one of those debates. Natalie didn't know how to 'get buck' as Bubo says. You and Keisha at least know how to argue with opponents and have some kind of instincts when to go after certain things. You think Natalie could have won that Towson debate tonight?"

Darren nodded in agreement with what I said, so I continued on. "There is so much stupid stuff said in these debates. From now on, if these other teams say something idiotic or unethical or they lie, you have to shut it down!"

"Shut it down!" Darren exclaimed. Preston and Doug also joined in and all three yelled out, "Shut it down!"

"As for you two," I said, pointing at Preston and Doug. "You have to help out Amber and Sandra with these other teams. Last year a bunch of teams said terrible things to our female debaters, and you guys need to be there to ensure shit like that doesn't happen again."

We kept chatting and drinking into the A.M., until there was no more Yuengling left. With Doc's departure, I felt one thing we lacked was fiery motivational speeches, and maybe I felt obliged to do some of them. Or maybe I was venting after what had been quite the ordeal traveling to the tourney. Either way, that night in Winston-Salem was one of the most memorable times I ever had with the U of L debate team.

Once again, none of the varsity teams made elims at Wake Forest. The strategy wasn't connecting with judges, and I wasn't sure the duos were connecting with each other. The novices, however, cruised through the tourney at Appalachian State. I didn't see the initial elim rounds there, but when the dust was settled, the finals of the novice tourney saw Preston and Sandra vs. the suit-wearing pricks from Vanderbilt. This time we were ready for them. All Preston had to do was read the Staudenmeier card I gave him.

One of the hotel rooms was converted into a debate room for the novice finals. Sure enough, Vandy launched into their speciesism 1AC, which I figured they would do. Sandra ran her 1NC speech on white-ness. Vandy countered with their 2AC, and now I was waiting with bated breath for Preston's 2NC where he would put the dagger in these geeks once and for all. Some of our team was stunned when Preston opened with a "road map," which in debate terms is a preview of main points in a speech. U of L loathed road maps, feeling it led to judges compartmentalizing arguments. I waited...and waited...and Preston never read the Staudenmeier card.

As prep time began, I pulled Bubo into the hotel room bathroom and closed the door. This was the angriest I'd ever been while watching one of our debates.

"What the hell is Preston doing out there? Why didn't he read the anti-speciesism card I gave him?" I ranted.

"We're fine, don't worry about it," Bubo said, laughing. I shook my head in disbelief.

But we weren't fine. I don't even remember the rebuttals. They didn't matter anyway. Once the judges deliberated, they came back with the verdict: 2–1 Vanderbilt. The swing judge said, "The Louisville team nearly had my ballot, but what I think you guys needed was something to explain why speciesism is offensive to your own philosophy. Maybe something noting the crazed extremism of some of these PETA types." Dammit! We had that debate won. To quote Dennis Green, "They were who we thought they were, and we let them off the hook!"

I was fuming the entire trip home. I never even turned on the radio, but instead burned a hole in Preston and Doug's ears about what happened in the final debate all through North Carolina, Virginia, and most of West Virginia. I think I wanted to beat Vanderbilt worse than them.

"Preston, why didn't you read the Staudenmeier evidence I gave you? It cost us the debate," I wondered.

"Bubo and Miriam told me not to listen to you. They didn't want the debate to go in that direction. I should have read the card anyway."

"They said *what*?" I asked indignantly. "They told you to ignore me? The Staudenmeier card fits perfectly with our team's principles! As far as I'm concerned, I gave you what you needed to win that debate. They gave you what you needed to lose it."

Preston changed the subject and launched into more of his libertarian spiel after we passed a few toll booths in West Virginia. "The interstate system should be privatized. It would be better run and people would gain more out of it."

"Take a look around you, Preston. We are driving in the middle of nowhere in West Virginia and soon eastern Kentucky. What company would maintain roads around here expecting any sort of profit? To me, taking more and more away from the people and putting everything in the hands of a few rich guys is a sort of corporate fascism waiting to happen." Not to be outdone, Preston then launched into a tirade against traffic lights and stop signs, as well as his disdain for Keynesian economics and the minimum wage, and I tuned him out.

After Wake Forest, I became nihilistic in my view of the program. I risked life and limb for this team, was tired, mentally exhausted, and my input wasn't valued whatsoever. By the time we got to Huntington, we stopped for gas. I mellowed out when I ran into John Williams in the gas station.

"Man, that flat tire was crazy," he said. "I know what it's like to make this trip back home to D.C. West Virginia scares me. It's nothing but people out of *The Hills Have Eyes*."

I laughed at John's remark.

Preston grabbed some massive thirty-two-ounce cans of malt liquor, enough for him, Doug, Darren, and me. Darren got in the car with us for the first time. Apparently, Darren and Preston had bonded over their mutual love of weed.

As we crossed back into Kentucky and saw the freaky Marathon oil refinery off I-64, it was a signal for the guys to bust out the malt liquor. Once we cruised past Ashland, Preston also passed around his weed, somewhat to my chagrin.

"Are you actually smoking weed in the car? Don't do that! At least roll down the windows!" I implored. They didn't quit smoking, but they rowed down the windows. Soon after we caught up to Bubo's minivan. As we ran neck and neck, I motioned to her as if to say, "Wanna race?"

It was a dark night, I-64 looked empty, and we were in the middle of nowhere in eastern Kentucky, so she seemed to take me up on my offer. We both revved up our engines for a race, but it didn't last long. After a few seconds, something seemed wrong with the minivan, so Bubo pulled off to the side of the road. I stopped as well. It was nothing serious, so she started back up again, but we didn't attempt any further drag racing. We didn't arrive back in Louisville until after midnight. I drank my can of malt liquor a couple of days later. I've never tried it again.

The rest of the semester consisted of finishing up classes. I spent the downtime going over to my mom's and drinking beer every night with my brother, Eric. My second year with U of L debate was the closest I've ever come to being an alcoholic. The combination of stress from graduate-level classes and dealing with the debate team had driven me to drink. The late-night drunken camaraderie had brought our group together at Wake Forest, so there became a tendency to push things as far as we could. What could possibly go wrong? The Spring 2011 semester was destined to be a wild, out-of-control time period for the Malcolm X Debate Team. Whether it would be a successful one or not was unclear.

CHAPTER 12

COLLEGE DEBATE IS DECADENT AND DEPRAVED

The squad dedicated the January debate team retreat to figuring out what we needed to do to start winning at the varsity level. The changes made to the strategy involved focusing on the Black/White binary and applying it to debate, as well as trying to advocate for which team could best exemplify ethos, pathos, and logos in a debate. This was in addition to the usual whiteness. I don't know if I agreed with the binary aspect.

I could already see an Asian or Hispanic debater skewering it by saying, "I don't fit into either side of the binary. By trying to fit me into being Black/White, you aren't trying to understand my experience at all."

We pressed forward, regardless. One amusing moment saw Bubo read a passage from a whiteness journal article that said something about "the army of whiteness."

Within seconds, Preston sent a text message saying, "The armies of whiteness!!!"

"I know. I know," I replied.

One of the main necessities involved finding Vicky McDonald a new partner, which wasn't difficult. For much of the Fall 2010 semester, Ryan Hugo, a slightly heavyset blonde guy, popped in here and there to say hi to Bubo and Marlene. I believe he debated on the team at one point and was looking to come back to school. He was somewhat of a techie type, so I initially feared he might be gunning for my GTA spot, but later realized he was still an undergrad. Thus, he gladly rejoined the team and become Vicky's partner. For those keeping track, the team now had four white male debaters (Ryan, Doug, Preston, Carl), which struck me as curious for a team focused on dismantling whiteness. Ryan and Carl were true believers, though, whereas Preston and Doug weren't. I agreed in principle with some of our strategy, but felt it was deployed in a faulty manner.

The team itself wasn't unified, but instead had several cliques. Bubo's group had Miriam, Josie (when she was around), Keisha, and Vicky. My group consisted of Preston, Doug, and later Darren. Carl, John, and Ryan roomed together on the road. Amber and Sandra did their own thing but also could veer in and out of Bubo's group and also sometimes needed to spend time with Preston and Doug on the road to go over strategy.

I was never part of Bubo's inner circle. She never confided in me about any intrigue going on in her life, and more frustratingly sometimes never sent me much needed texts. For instance, if a squad meeting was cancelled, sometimes I didn't receive a text and sat in the squad room alone working on class assignments or posting debates on YouTube.

Bubo and I had a peculiar dynamic by early 2011. She was a classmate of mine in Quantitative Methods that semester, so while she was technically my boss in the debate room, she also sometimes asked me for help with class. When we went to tourneys, I suppose I could have been considered the number two person in the debate program, which is kind of a sad statement. I was a second-year grad assistant while Miriam was in her first year.

For some unfathomable reason, the next tournament had us traveling once again to Navy. After the debacle of the previous year, I couldn't imagine why we would think of going back there, but

SALVAGED FROM THE FLOOD

thankfully we flew into Baltimore. My new bag, a Christmas gift from my girlfriend Amanda, was torn to shreds by the baggage machine, so the staff handed me a brand-new piece of luggage and an apology from the airport. Of course, we got lost yet again, almost ending up in downtown Baltimore before turning around, as Preston joked, "That's the problem with this team. We don't believe in road maps."

When we arrived at our seedy motel, I walked into my room and noticed huge cockroaches all over the floor. I ran out in a hurry and noticed other people freaking out as well. Bubo went back to the office and informed the manager we would not be staying there. Marlene, ever the Penelope Garcia of the team, managed to secure a refund from this flophouse and instead booked us into the much nicer Doubletree down the road.

Preston and I ventured out to find a nearby liquor store to load up for this tourney. Annapolis has cameras on every street corner, enough to make someone paranoid. It's also insanely cold in January. My feet never thawed out the entire trip. The hotel room was even cold, and I couldn't figure out why. Doug and I were now sharing the same bed, with Preston and Darren in the other. I laid down the ground rule that I didn't want to see any marijuana, to which Darren responded, "Hell, I brought some weed with me on the plane today. No one cared. I wasn't searched."

The tournament at Navy went smoother than the previous year, but alas, it wasn't very successful. The 2010 Navy event almost destroyed the entire team, so being marginal with whiteness and the Black/White binary arguments was a step up. In a fascinating turn of events, Rhett Barrett (half of the Liberty married couple we encountered the prior year) voted for Williams/Vance.

"I went into that elim round last year knowing we were likely going to win given those judges, but maybe we shouldn't have," Rhett said. I picked the Barretts up (voted for them) in the debate I judged, which didn't hurt.

"I remember judging you all last year. If I recall, your wife bailed you out with her last speech," I said. He laughed as we built an unlikely coalition.

We couldn't get around the fact that Navy was not a good tournament for U of L. Towson, despite being a few miles down the road from Annapolis, didn't even bother to compete at Navy. After the first day, the varsity duos were once again treading water, with the novices being decent but not faring as well as other tournaments.

Preston seemed troubled at this tourney. Late at night and still drinking, he unloaded a jarring bombshell that he had impregnated a girl during his first sexual experience and her subsequent abortion haunted him similar to part of the song "The Freshmen." Before we left to check out and head to Navy for the elim round, Preston walked over and shut the window behind the drapes in the hotel room.

"You dick! That's why I've been freezing this entire trip!" I said.

Even with the angst, Preston and Sandra were the only U of L team to make elims at Navy, which again posed a problem since we had a plane to catch. In this case, the debate was a ho-hum round against George Mason, which we lost 3–0. What were these judges going to do, vote for us at Navy? The judges didn't care for Preston's chart drawing bit, feeling it did nothing to deconstruct whiteness.

We rushed to the airport but made it on time. The four of us found a sports bar and attempted to watch the Bears/Packers NFC title game on a plasma TV with a terrible burn in. Preston was strapped for cash, and somehow convinced Doug to pay for another beer. What blew my mind was why the waitress allowed it. She let the underage Doug buy a beer as long as it was for the twenty-two-year-old Preston, which I have to admit I have never seen before. By the end of the day, Doug would be saddened by his Jets losing the AFC title game to the Steelers. Preston attempted to console him.

"Come on, Doug. You know Mark Sanchez sucks."

The UK tournament in Lexington was next on the docket, which took place over Super Bowl weekend. After a respite from speciesism, Vanderbilt was back in full force. I still don't think the novices ran the

Staudenmeier card I gave them, which continued to baffle me since I felt it could clearly beat speciesism.

I made a point of checking out Vicky and Ryan's debates, and I quickly learned Hugo engaged in some epic white self-loathing. Most of his speeches involved ranting "white people suck, Black Power!" and things of that nature.

Even Deven Cooper took issue with some of his rhetoric while judging a round vs. Mary Washington, asking, "So do you want to cause harm to whites or something?" This coming from a guy who won a CEDA national championship doing the Black Rage/Kill Whitey argument.

I felt sorry for Vicky. She went from having a deer-in-the-headlights partner to a guy primarily concerned with bashing his own racial group. There's a difference between acknowledging historical white dominance in society and white self-hatred, and Hugo often crossed into the latter in my view. I liked Vicky as a human being, and joked around with her in the debate room, talked about wrestling, anything that came to mind. But I never saw what she was capable of in debate. At times I think she expected judges and opponents to understand everything she said without expounding on her evidence.

Later that night, Preston went on the town in Lexington with some UK friends, even checking in on Facebook at a club so everyone on the team knew he had snuck out.

Both novice teams lost yet again to Vanderbilt at UK, as the Vandy novices shut down the entire tourney by having co-winners. This was mighty frustrating. I knew we could beat them, but we weren't doing what needed to be done to crush this speciesism nonsense once and for all.

After their elim round loss to Vanderbilt, a frustrated Amber cornered one of the suit-wearing Vandy guys. She let him know how she felt about their strategy. "Do you really believe any of this speciesism stuff? Do you even know how hurtful it is to hear my plight as an African American compared to animals?"

"It's our strategy and we think it has some merit. Nothing personal," he replied.

A group of us ran into Deven Cooper during lunch. He asked how we had been doing and I responded, "Lost to Vanderbilt on speciesism. Again."

"You are still losing to that bullshit?" he asked. "We lost to speciesism once at Towson, and I said, 'never again' and found some Tim Wise evidence burying speciesism. There's plenty of criticisms out there. Tell yourself it won't happen again." In one conversation, I now understood the difference between what we were doing and what Towson was doing.

The debating continued into the Super Bowl itself, which I found insane. The last debate of the tourney was another McDonald/Hugo debate against a team from Minnesota who waxed poetic about the virtues of Hugo Chavez's Venezuela. This was some laughable stuff, but again, our debaters were trained not to directly answer another team. In this debate, Hugo flew off the handle at the Minnesota team and in his final speech finished by saying, "So, in closing, I will give you a hearty 'fuck you!'"

Before the judgment came down, I turned to Bubo and asked, "If these two guys are so thrilled with Hugo Chavez, why don't they move to Venezuela and see how much they enjoy themselves?" She shook her head and laughed. The judge ruled for Minnesota. Doug tried to watch the Super Bowl on his laptop, relaying the score during prep time.

After the rounds ended, Preston insisted on going out for more beer. Finding a store open late on Super Bowl Sunday proved difficult. We finally found a grocery store that had what he wanted, then went back and watched the rest of the game in the hotel room. Preston wasn't interested in the game, noting, "The Cowboys aren't in it, so who cares?"

We had our own Super Bowl party in the hotel room. Beyond the four of us, some random people from other teams even came to the room, since for once we had a multi-room suite and a terrific bathroom with a huge tub. Doug was trashed at this party, and we started discussing recent TNA wrestling storylines.

"I dunno, man. I can't believe these morons thought turning Jeff Hardy heel would be a good idea," I said.

"I used to like TNA when they were first on Spike, but once they signed Kurt Angle, the show became a WWE knockoff and I stopped caring," a bleary-eyed Doug retorted. For the record, the Packers won the game over the Steelers, 31–25, but I think most of us were wasted by the time the game ended. Yet again, our group left a hotel room a mess filled with empty beer bottles. Debating was getting in the way of our partying.

To add to our woes, the next day the weather turned bad right as we had to leave. Only seventy miles separate Louisville and Lexington, but with snow and ice falling, the trip became a lot scarier. A massive wreck shut down I-64 somewhere around Frankfort. We traveled in one big van on this occasion, with Miriam driving, so with no other recourse, Miriam turned the van around and drove the opposite way down the interstate until she found the previous exit. I'd never experienced something that wild before. Even with the Evel Knievel antics, we ran into a traffic jam on the back roads. We left after eating breakfast, but didn't get back until 4:00 p.m. This marked the third time I almost died on a debate trip. Navy in early 2010, Wake Forest in November 2010, and UK in February 2011.

We had a few weeks to prepare for the ADA tournament at Emory in Atlanta. Bubo planned a curious experiment. The idea had two of our coaches, Miriam and Josie, face off with two of the varsity debaters, Carl and John. The debaters were going to grab random evidence out of folders and read it while the coaches ran our whiteness strategy.

I was at the end of my rope dealing with Vanderbilt and speciesism. Since Miriam was preparing for the practice debate, I felt the need to discuss a few things over lunch one day with Doug and Preston. We went over to the Humanities Building for some privacy away from the team. I started discussing potential strategies.

"Guys, we may only have one more tourney against Vanderbilt.

You need to start using the Staudenmeier evidence I gave you. That card and whatever else you can find bashing speciesism is the key to beating them."

"I'm over this whole whiteness thing," Doug said dejectedly. "Me and my good friend whiteness want to go home. This isn't what I signed up for."

"What did you expect this to be, Doug?" I asked. "Once I saw the team website and saw the headline 'Malcolm X Debate Team,' I knew what the program was going to be."

"I've had enough," Preston said. "I'm going to run the Staudenmeier card at Emory. It can't hurt. We've already been losing to them."

"Believe me, I know you guys are frustrated. Every school is losing to Vanderbilt in these novice rounds. But let's get real. They have VM Zardoz, one of the premier Directors of Debate in the country. They have Cindy Bader as one of their main coaches. Carter Morris takes great amusement in beating U of L. On our side there's Bubo, thrust into being interim Director of Debate. Miriam was up and down as a debater to say the least. And you have me, and I have no idea what the hell I'm doing. I'm not saying you can't be friends with the Vandy squad later on Facebook. But at Emory, you have to go all out."

A few days later, the big practice debate took place in the debate room. I filmed the debate for future reference. Miriam and Josie dusted off their old speeches and read them with a new slant on the current strategy, while Carl Vance and John Williams read random cards from our evidence folders. Vicky McDonald judged. The scary thing? Carl and John won this debate decisively. If there was ever an indictment of our varsity strategy, this was it.

The trip to Atlanta went smoothly, but all the trips we had made to Georgia seemed to go the smoothest. That may account for why I have no problem driving back to Atlanta even today, whereas I have vowed to never set foot in West Virginia ever again. I've almost died every time I've gone through there. And, yes, Preston and I stocked up on beer. At this tournament, however, I realized all of this drunken debauchery was starting to get out of hand.

I hadn't seen much of Carl and John all year, maybe a few debates here and there. For whatever reason, they weren't holding my interest. I decided to rectify that at the ADAs and picked a highly contentious round against two girls from West Georgia. This debate turned into a complete dumpster fire. John, as per usual, used some colorful language in the debate and the West Georgia team took exception to his casual use of the n-word in the debate. As a Black male, he felt he could use it, but when they used it to voice their concerns, John totally lost his mind. He invoked the images of lynched Black men hanging from trees, crosses burning, and told them to fuck off. They had a typically West Georgia response.

"They may be offended by our use of a certain word, but we are also upset at their use of 'fuck' in this debate. It is a form of verbal violence, and we protest its usage."

I didn't envy Hank Avera having to judge this mess. At the end of the decision, he awarded the ballot to West Georgia because we hadn't addressed the rest of their debate, and the whole n-word vs. fuck aspect was a wash on a judge's flow. I recorded all of this debate. I wish I hadn't.

This debate showcased the main problem Carl and John had as a team, namely there was no real leader. The previous year John had Josie to reign him in and Carl did his own stuff while deferring to Miriam. Carl now deferred to the senior John, but at times John had the wrong instincts. The varsity teams that year didn't mesh. Carl and John never clicked, Keisha was dragging Darren down, and Vicky had one partner quit and had to try to figure out another.

After the round, West Georgia coach Ruby Boyer approached me in the hall. An old school hippie feminist type, I was interested in what she had to say.

"What went on in that round just now?" she asked. "My team seemed upset by it."

"So was I. That entire debate should have never happened. The whole debate turned into a war of 'Who said what bad word?' and it was embarrassing to watch. I apologize on behalf of our team because I think John went off the deep end. I understand why he ranted at what your team said, and they shouldn't have said that word, but I don't think what he did was at all constructive."

"Hey, it's cool. These things can happen. I'm going to have a conversation with my team about their role in the debate," Ruby said.

Aside from that fiasco, the varsity teams finished the first day hovering around .500 yet again. The novices were running the Staudenmeier evidence and beat Vanderbilt decisively in both meetings. Preston and Sandra were unbeaten after the first day, Doug and Amber 2–1.

Back at the hotel, Preston, Doug, and Darren tore loose to celebrate the great day the novices had. I drank two beers as usual and tried to go to bed, but the other guys kept drinking. And drank some more. They sneaked into the bathroom and covered the vent in order to smoke weed. I told them previously I didn't want to see them with marijuana or I'd have to tell Bubo. I have no idea when they went to sleep, or if they got any sleep.

In the morning, Preston was in no condition to debate. In fact, he even drank *another* beer right before we left to eat breakfast and head to the tourney. I started to think I had created a monster here. In the first debate of the day, I sat in on the round with Preston and Sandra against the other Vanderbilt novice team who Doug and Amber had defeated the day before. Preston ran out of the room and vomited in a trash can during prep time.

"Is Preston okay?" one of the Vandy guys asked. Obviously that round was a loss, ditto the next. After lunch, he sobered up enough to win the last debate, as Preston and Sandra finished 4–2 and needed to focus on elims the next day.

That night, the guys seemed to chill out. There was still a little beer drinking, but nowhere near as crazy as the previous night. In fact, the topic of conversation turned to Vanderbilt coach Cindy Bader.

"This will sound odd, but Cindy Bader talked to me between rounds the other day and I could swear she was hitting on me," Darren said.

"I think she's barking up the wrong tree there, but yeah, I've heard she is into Black men," I replied. Darren had a white girlfriend in high school, this being before he came out as gay.

"I'd bang her if I had the chance, though," Preston chimed in with his thoughts on the well-endowed Bader.

"Yeah, you would say that, Preston," I said. "I knew you would be into the evil hot debate coach chicks. Maybe you'll run into Gretchen Stedman at CEDA? But, gentlemen, I think it's time for a toast. What should we toast to?"

"To whiteness!" Darren yelled. We all had a drink.

"To speciesism!" Preston exclaimed. We had another drink.

"To winning this tourney tomorrow!" Doug bellowed. One last drink.

"And to Cindy Bader's tits," I quietly added. Everyone spit out their beer in laughter.

The novices competed in elims the next day. Bubo informed me Miriam was presently in no condition to drive back, since she had been partying way too hard the previous night as well. This revelation confirmed a suspicion of mine, namely that my guys weren't the only ones getting trashed on a regular basis after a day of debating.

When the dust settled in the novice bracket, Preston and Sandra made the finals against the suit-wearing pricks from Vanderbilt. One last debate against these guys. I thought we were ready for them. There was one problem. The minute the first Vandy guy launched into his 1AC, I realized they had completely changed strategies. He never mentioned speciesism once in nine minutes. Sandra, for her part, wasn't rattled and pulled off her usual whiteness spiel, but Preston was thrown for a loop. He never recovered and kept harping on speciesism even though Vanderbilt wasn't running it in that round.

Instead, Vanderbilt's strategy insisted we were *extra* topical instead of off topic since we had both topical immigration evidence as well as whiteness evidence. They knew everyone accused U of L of not being predictable, so they could get away with not being predictable themselves. One of them threw in some barbs directed at me as I filmed the debate.

"These debates are so heated, what would happen if either of our administrations saw this stuff? Some programs have even been shut down like Fort Hays State."

Given some of our debates, that comment hit close to home.

This one wasn't close. The judges returned the decision 3–0 for Vanderbilt. That debate was the last time we faced off with them, and the novices never beat them in an elim round. Regardless, one would be hard-pressed to find better novice debates anywhere in the country than the ones U of L had with Vanderbilt in 2010–11.

Miriam was coherent enough by the time we left to drive back home, though we stopped a couple of times at fast food restaurants for her to get her bearings. The mood was light on the trip back, with no need to be mad. They had screwed us by changing strategies to something we hadn't seen. Doug and I chuckled at some of Preston's sillier moments in the debate.

"I especially enjoyed when Preston screwed up and said something about 'the flowers of whiteness...no, wait, the thorns of whiteness!'" I cracked. "And why did you let them go after me for filming the debate?"

"I love you, Brian," Doug said.

"Well, I'm glad to hear it, Doug. After all, we've been sleeping together on and off for months," I jested.

I turned on the radio as we entered Chattanooga, to some '80s channel playing REO Speedwagon's "Can't Fight This Feeling." Of course, we changed the lyrics and sang in unison. "I can't fight this whiteness anymore...I've forgotten what I started fighting whiteness for..." We had one more tournament left to go, and since no one had the required points to make the National Debate Tournament (NDT), CEDA was the team's most important event in a long time. It was a make-or-break moment for the entire program.

CHAPTER 13

MARCH IN BINGHAMTON

The varsity teams didn't sweat the upcoming CEDA tournament. At this stage there was no point changing the entire strategy, so there were some minor tweaks at most. Most of the debaters seemed weary of whiteness as well.

"I'm doing one more tournament with whiteness, but after CEDA, I'm done with it. I've looked into the quare thing you mentioned and next year I might want to run some of that," Darren said during the week we prepared for CEDA.

The novices changed some things around. Since Vanderbilt's novices weren't competing at CEDA, we didn't worry about speciesism anymore. I was largely hands off at this point and let Miriam coach them up. I tried to finish my classes in order to graduate and also had comprehensive exams after we returned from CEDA. Some of the changes were notable. Preston dropped the chart drawing bit and instead started using music such as "A Whole New World" from *Aladdin* ("I want to show you a whole new world without whiteness"). Doug also started using music as well, John Mayer's "Waiting on the World to Change," which is more self-explanatory. More importantly, the novices started hammering home the Peggy McIntosh whiteness checklist from *Unpacking the Invisible Knapsack*.

We had a final team get together about a week before we left for the CEDA tournament in Binghamton, NY. Everyone met up at Keisha's parents' house slightly south of Fern Creek. I quite liked Keisha's parents, and her dad didn't mind if I rummaged through his R & B and jazz record collection. Truth be told, I liked Keisha as well. She was a nice person outside of debate rounds, but debating had made her more and more unhappy during tournaments. The entire evening confirmed my suspicions that Keisha came from a privileged background.

The squad left for Binghamton on Friday, March 18. The city was a random place to host the biggest college debate tournament in the country. Binghamton was a strange city, with an atmosphere that transported one back in time. The storefronts and overall atmosphere seemed like something out of the 1950s or early '60s, similar to the movie *American Graffiti*, minus the classic cars.

We stayed at the tournament hotel, the Riverwalk, nestled on the banks of the Chenango River. It was the best hotel we stayed at in the two years I traveled with the team. My room had a charming riverfront view, and for once we stayed in a hotel that had a decent swimming pool, hot tub, and even a sauna room. I also had my own room again. Maybe the team had more money for CEDA, or maybe Bubo felt the need to separate our group of doom. Either way, the first thing Preston and I did was find the nearest restaurant, the Lost Dog Café, and of course Preston wanted to go to the liquor store next door. He wasn't even messing around with beer anymore, but instead bought some whiskey and a shot glass.

The squad had one final pre-tourney meeting in Bubo's room to go over last-minute strategy ideas. Preston brought the bottle of whiskey and the shot glass to the meeting and spent the entire meeting downing shots right in front of Bubo and the entire team. I couldn't help but think Preston was trying to burn bridges by now. Nothing short of winning the novice tournament would save his spot on the team.

The main four of us headed back to my room for a while and had a few beers. Once again, I offered a toast.

"Here's to hopefully winning this thing," I said as they took a drink. "Oh, and to Cindy Bader's tits."

"And Cindy Bader's tits!" Preston, Doug, and Darren said in unison.

The tournament started early Saturday morning. I judged the first round of the day, a tilt between Ryan Wash and LaToya Williams-Green of Emporia State against a Towson team I hadn't seen before. Wash was an impressive speaker, but the crux of the debate involved this Towson team using a peculiar soccer metaphor that I felt didn't clash with Emporia's affirmative. This was a rare early round debate with a captivated audience, as well as the only time I didn't vote for Towson. I couldn't help but think this Wash guy had a future, and indeed he did. In 2013, Wash and Elijah Smith became the only team to ever win both CEDA and the NDT in the same year.

Thankfully, I received a respite from judging in the second half of the day and decided to check out Darren and Keisha's debate against another Towson team I hadn't seen, a Hispanic duo. Ruby Boyer judged the round, so I felt we had a decent chance. This Towson team seemed oddly cheerful and performed a routine where they wore white masks and took them off mid-debate as some sort of metaphor they never quite explained. Thankfully, Darren and Keisha felt where the debate needed to go, realized they had a radical hippie like Boyer judging, and executed a "Power to the People!" debate that won them the ballot. This debate made me realize U of L had nothing to fear vs. Towson teams, as long as we knew when to shift either to the center or hard left.

I checked out the novices as well. Preston's and Doug's attempts at playing music met with some resistance from judges. After one round, a judge scolded Preston's *Aladdin* music, saying, "What company could be more entrenched in whitewashing other cultures than Disney?" Doug's John Mayer song also didn't go over well with another judge, who brought up Mayer's interview a year earlier where he said his "penis was a white supremacist." Doug, who hadn't read this interview, freaked out and vowed to never use Mayer's song again.

After the first day, the varsity teams performed decently enough, hovering around 2–2. The novices struggled, which was to be expected since they were now facing a decent amount of varsity teams since CEDA is an open tournament. Regardless of being placed in another room, Preston and Doug came up to my room to hang out after the tough day of debating. I tried to reign these guys in, but this was CEDA and even if they weren't drinking in the room with me, they could get drunk anywhere else, including at an open bar downstairs in the hotel.

The next day started with me having to judge another Towson debate. The round featured Ben Crossan and Fernando Kirkman against a wacky UT San Antonio team. The other Towson/UTSA debate I judged was the most uncomfortable debate I could imagine, but thankfully this one was zany and amusing. Darren and Keisha ran into this UTSA team the previous day and lost to them. UTSA ran a wild strategy advocating that the federal government should expand visas for vampires. Darren and Keisha let these guys stay in a metaphorical world, but Crossan and Kirkman allowed them no such luxury. They pointed out the inherent absurdity of the argument, keeping the debate grounded in reality. This was a no-brainer Towson win. Crossan and Kirkman were one of the best teams in the field.

I decided to check out Carl and John next. The duo faced a novice Liberty team that would soon become a bigger part of this tournament. What fascinated me about Max Holman and Nick Mueller was that they professed an interest in debating whiteness, a shocking turn of events for the usually conservative Liberty. Since this was a varsity/novice debate, it wasn't a particularly fair fight as Carl and John waxed these two. We would see Holman and Mueller again, however.

Since I didn't judge again, I finished the day watching Doug and Amber against Clarion, with Ruby Boyer judging. The most memorable thing about the debate was Doug had now replaced John Mayer with John Lennon's "Imagine." Even though Boyer voted for us in the debate, she chastised Doug for his music choices.

"What am I as a woman to think of the gendered language in that song?" Hilariously, since opponents never listened to the songs and didn't engage them, poor song choices didn't cost us debates.

After the prelim rounds were over, all of U of L's varsity teams once again finished 5–3 at CEDA and made the elims. U of L did well at CEDA because of a combination of friendlier judges and facing a couple of novice teams who couldn't handle our arguments. The novices struggled more, both finishing 3–5 but qualifying for the novice breakout tournament, a tourney of the top eight novice teams in the field. Other qualifiers included two Liberty teams, in particular Holman and Mueller.

Bubo decided to take the team to a soul food restaurant to celebrate everyone making elims. We drove aimlessly around downtown Binghamton, getting lost as usual. Preston, Doug, and Darren were riding with me, and after about the third turnaround, I finally lost my mind. In a regrettable moment, I ranted, "These Black women can't drive for shit!" Darren, for his part, wasn't happy.

"I take offense to that, Brian. I don't appreciate it."

I cooled down and apologized. "I'm sorry, Darren. But we get lost on every trip and I'm sick of it." The restaurant was closed anyway since it was late on a Sunday night.

The four of us took an elevator back up to our various rooms. On the way up, Darren stopped me and wanted to discuss what had happened in the car further.

"You know, I have been thinking about this, but didn't Doc get us lost in downtown Baltimore last year and not Bubo?"

"Yeah, that's right," I replied. "But then someone could counter and say, 'Both Black men and Black women can't drive for shit.'"

Darren chuckled, realizing I permed his argument the way so many teams had permed us all year. We then headed over to Carl and John's room, and I noticed they had some Crown Royal on the desk. I wasn't surprised.

What also didn't surprise me was the next day's results. In what should be a shock to no one, all of the U of L varsity teams lost in their respective elimination rounds. I don't even remember any of those debates because I focused more on what was going on with the novice division. Doug and Amber defeated another Liberty team in the Elite 8 round, while Preston and Sandra defeated James Madison in their round. Preston had a surprisingly touching moment before the decision was announced.

"If this decision doesn't go our way, I just wanted you to know I have enjoyed having you as a partner this year," he said.

The decision was 2–1, U of L. Thus, the semis were set for the next day. Doug and Amber vs. Case Western, while Preston and Sandra were going to face Holman and Mueller from Liberty.

By this point we ran out of beer again, so Preston and I made a trip to another liquor store to load up for the rest of the tournament. After all, the next day was the last day of the tournament and there surely would be a massive party. We wanted to be ready. After leaving the store, Preston asked, "Can we go by the Days Inn and pick up some-one? I met this girl from Illinois State at lunch today and told her about the open bar at the Riverwalk." I was slightly miffed at this, but eventually agreed. We picked up this girl at the Days Inn and took her back to the Riverwalk. After taking our haul up to my fridge I headed downstairs to the open bar.

The bar was packed with debaters, and they weren't exactly carding anyone. I ran into Crossan and Kirkman, and while we had a beer together, we all joked about their debate with UTSA. "I couldn't believe those guys with the vampire 1AC. In my decision I said, 'What would Buffy think of what you are suggesting?'"

Ben and Fernando both laughed, with Fernando reiterating, "What would Buffy *think*?" On the way back to my hotel room, I shared the elevator with one of the UTSA guys and it took a serious effort not to laugh.

At about 2 A.M., a furious knock on the door woke me up. I opened it to find Preston and Doug.

"Brian, let us in," Doug whispered. "We had to get away from something that is going on in our room."

I was confused, but let them in. They crashed on the bed and I slept in the chair. As I found out later, Darren was entertaining one Ahmed Griffith, a former champion debater who was back coaching and judging at the tourney. I met Ahmed at CEDA the year before when he judged one of our debates. While I don't have a particularly good gaydar, Ahmed's preferences were easy to figure out after about twenty seconds.

Tuesday was the last day of the tournament. Rounds were held at the Riverwalk instead of on campus since spring break had ended and classes were back in session. Banquet rooms and even the bar were used for various debates. Our novice teams debated at the same time. Since Doug and Amber's opponent didn't intrigue me, I checked out Preston and Sandra against Liberty.

By this point, Holman and Mueller were quite into whiteness arguments and their idea was to beat us at our own game. They saw fit to play CeeLo Green's radio edit of "Forget You" before the debate instead of the more notorious "Fuck You" version. Quite appropriate since Liberty's attempt to run a whiteness argument was a sanitized, radio edit version of a whiteness debate. I wish we had used it against them. By this point, Preston and Sandra had dropped the music and most topical discussion in favor of the Peggy McIntosh checklist. Holman seemed interested in all of this, and I started thinking maybe they weren't doing a blatant co-opting of our strategy, after all. The debate was close, and the judges came back with the decision after a few minutes.

It was 2–1, Liberty. Preston and Sandra had been eliminated. Soon after, everyone in the room tried to find out what happened with Doug and Amber's debate, and sure enough, they won. So we still had them in the finals. In between the semis and finals, Bubo sent me to buy the team some Chinese food for lunch, and Preston went with me.

"I fear the same debate is going to happen with Doug and Amber," I said. "We can beat those guys and beat them decisively, but I'm worried the judges might listen to their more traditional version of what we are doing."

Preston, bummed out over the loss, didn't have much to say for once.

The novice finals were now set. I filmed the debate as usual, which took place in the smaller banquet room being used for the novices. The main varsity tourney used the bigger hall. We knew what they were going to do, and they knew what we were going to do. There wasn't much time for adjustments. Doug and Amber ran the same Peggy McIntosh evidence that Preston and Sandra used, albeit with a different set of judges. Holman amused me somewhat by talking about "Peggy" throughout the debate, as if he knew her. This debate closely resembled the semifinal to be honest. The final result was up to the judges.

I have never been more anxious than I was while awaiting that decision. The wait took an eternity, a time during which I reflected on all the chaos of the past year. Dr. Bedford's bizarre departure, the various road woes, all the losses to Vanderbilt, everything the team had endured. After a long wait, the judges announced their decision.

It was 2–1, Louisville.

Wait, hold on. Did they say 2–1, *Louisville?* We won? We won! Oh my God, we won! Doug Lusco and Amber Burns won the CEDA Novice National Championship! I fumbled the camera while it was still recording because I started applauding so enthusiastically. Bubo, Miriam, and the entire team surrounded the new champions as the room cleared. After all the close calls, we finally got one.

A celebration was in order. Bubo took the team to Red Lobster for a big "end of the year" meal. I sat at the table with Bubo, the novices, Darren, and of all people, Ahmed Griffith, who Bubo invited to come along. For once, we sat down without instinctively segregating ourselves, which had become a running joke throughout the year. During dinner, Ahmed made various thinly-veiled references to his time with Darren the previous night while Doug sat squirming in his seat.

"I have an idea for a satirical debate I might want to do," I mentioned. "I would be the most ultra whiteness debater ever. I'd bust out my dad's old crocodile Izod shirts, do nothing but quote Reagan, and my music choices would be Air Supply and early '80s Chicago."

"I love Peter Cetera!" Preston exclaimed.

"Of course, you do, Preston. Of course, you do," I replied.

Upon returning to the hotel, we watched most of the varsity championship round, the main event of the entire tourney. The championship round paired Towson's Crossan and Kirkman against Kansas State. Since Towson was debating, everyone from U of L wanted to watch, a stark contrast from the previous year when I was the only U of L person who bothered to represent the team during the Oklahoma/Whitman final. For the record, Kansas State won the title on a 6–3 decision (nine judges scored the final round). Whiteness lived to fight another day.

Later that evening we made some time to go to the pool, at least all the novices and me. Doug was exhausted by this point and sat in the hot tub relaxing, from time-to-time mumbling, "I can't believe we actually won." Preston, for his part, swam laps in a lane, trying to impress Amber and Sandra. We even made time to head to the sauna. I was excited to see that the Riverwalk had a swim trunk dryer in the sauna room area.

Doug was exhausted and crashed back in the room, but Preston and I found out about a party upstairs. The Vanderbilt team was hosting the party. Oddly enough, I don't think Vandy had a particularly great tournament overall. Preston tried to hit on a seriously drunk Cindy Bader, to which she said, "Preston, I am not going to bone you, so knock it off." Preston, being exhausted himself, left the party. For my part, I started talking to an also tipsy VM Zardoz, Vanderbilt's Director of Debate.

"I feel like this year U of L has tried to build some coalitions in the debate community. What sense is there in having everyone loathe you?" I asked. VM smiled, then took off the beaded necklace she was wearing around her neck and put it around mine. I smiled back at her and then turned to Cindy.

"Hey, look," Cindy said, reeling drunk. "I don't even care about this speciesism crap. It was all Carter Morris's idea."

"You know, Cindy, we don't really hate you, even though you may think we do. In fact, we've even been known to have toasts in your honor." After that wry comment, I left the party.

This being U of L debate, we couldn't have a nice, smooth trip back home the next day. The weather turned snowy, even in late March, and cancelled our flight out of Binghamton. We had no money left to go back to the hotel, and with no flights out of Binghamton in the near future, Marlene rerouted us to Syracuse. The flight wasn't until early the next morning, so we had to hang around the airport lobby the entire night.

Preston being Preston, called up this girl he knew named Madison. Even though she lived in Rochester about ninety miles away, Madison dropped everything to join us at the Syracuse airport. She even brought a twenty-four case of Natural Ice, the nastiest piss beer you'd ever want to drink. We spent the night drinking warm Natty Ice. I challenged Darren to a foot race in an empty hall of the airport, but he left me in the dust, and I crashed to the ground and rolled several feet. Darren had the build of a track star, so the challenge was foolish on my part.

Thankfully, the next morning we boarded our plane without further delay. At a brief layover in Chicago, Preston asked me to buy him a sausage biscuit at Wendy's.

"Don't you have any food money left?" I asked.

"Not really. I had to pay Madison back for the Natural Ice," he responded.

I spent the rest of the semester taking exams and editing footage for YouTube. The squad had an occasional post-tourney debate meeting. The plate-style trophy for the novice championship at CEDA took its place alongside other trophies and plaques in Davidson 101.

In the aftermath of our novices' triumph at CEDA, Bubo was named full-fledged Director of Debate for the 2011–12 year. Bubo's first act was to implement a stricter behavior code of conduct prohibiting underage drinking and drug use. Keisha Fisher was the first casualty of Bubo's stricter policy. As I heard later, she was kicked off the team the next year for rolling a joint in front of everyone in the debate room. Darren teamed with Carl after that.

Darren posted an emotional Facebook message in 2013 after he and Carl made the NDT, becoming U of L's first team to do so since 2005. Darren thanked everyone he knew on the U of L team over the years, but he left out my name. I can only assume he was still upset at my frustrated comment in the car in Binghamton, and I wish he knew how sorry I am now for having said it.

Doug Lusco stayed on with the U of L debate team for his entire college career, but after he graduated, I lost all track of him. I heard he took a job back in New York, but I haven't spoken to Doug in years.

And what of Preston Bates? In a shock to no one, Preston was not invited back to the debate team for the 2011–12 school year. I kept in touch with Preston for about a year, meeting up with him around Thanksgiving 2011 at the Granville Inn near campus. Preston had veered even harder into libertarian lunacy by then, rambling between drinks about the need for the U.S. to get rid of social security. My mother was a couple of years away from being on social security, so I became pissed at his suggestion and finally told him "shut the fuck up." I later invited him to come over and watch the 2012 NCAA tournament at my apartment, but he declined.

In 2012, Preston recruited Doug to join him working for John Ramsey's Liberty for All Super PAC, a Libertarian-Republican PAC. LFA spent a huge amount of money to get the bizarre Thomas Massie elected to Congress. I don't think Bubo advertises that a couple of her former debaters helped Massie win an election. Preston got a fair amount of coverage in the *Courier-Journal* in 2012. I have to admit, I came close to calling the newspaper to discredit him, given all I knew about his antics while with the debate program. I decided not to, because despite wanting to strangle him on occasion, I actually liked the guy. Over time, I lost touch with Preston. Today he runs an entrepreneur advising company.

Given the rise in prominence of race issues U of L's debate team discussed nearly twenty years ago, I can't help but think Dr. Bedford was a crazy visionary in his way. He is deserving of credit (or blame, depending on your point of view) for the discussion of race in modern-day America. He just had his demons and wasn't around to see his team's renewed success, along with the ideas he talked about becoming adopted by the mainstream. The discussions of whiteness, white privilege, and white supremacy are now a staple in American society, as is the politically heated debate over Critical Race Theory. The critics of CRT don't really understand much about it from what I've seen. I spent two years around some aspects of it and I don't fully understand it, so I can't see how a Republican politician would grasp it at all.

The team itself was threatened with extinction a few years after I graduated, when the communication department wanted to cut the program entirely from the yearly budget, but it was saved by the Pan-African studies department. I understood the communication department's frustration with the circumstances behind Dr. Bedford's questionable departure. Obviously I was known to rant about my own frustrations with the team to any professor in the department who would listen. The Malcom X Debate Society still exists to this day, with debaters achieving NDT accolades and Bubo winning coaching awards as well.

I viewed debate as a game when I was with the program, an act of competition to be analyzed and discussed. To be sure, I can envision members of the debate community viewing this piece about social activist debating as coming from a hetero white male perspective, to which I will plead guilty. In that case, I would encourage others to write their own experiences, to make themselves visible, to make themselves be heard.

Over the years, I have thought quite often about my time with the U of L debate team. Late at night while trying to fall asleep, I sometimes remember various rounds I judged, or silly moments in the debate room. In 2020, when George Floyd was killed and the raid on Breonna Taylor's apartment left her dead, the topics U of L, Towson, and other teams discussed crystallized in my head. I finally started to evaluate my own whiteness and the inherent privileges therein, the very sort of process Marlene implored me to do a decade earlier.

Many of the coaches and debaters at U of L viewed what they were doing as a movement, one that has grown with time. It started with one team shocking the debate world circa 2004, to a rising movement in the world of debate, and now a movement in society. I typically found fault with our strategy in the nuts and bolts of debate, but not the passion behind it. That passion has helped change the country.

Amber Burns and Doug Lusco. 2011 CEDA Novice National Champions. Photo courtesy of Amber Burns.

The remnants of the old Holiday Inn/Fern Valley Hotel near Fern Valley Road. I lived near the hotel until August 2012. The health department closed it in 2017.

Waverly Hills Sanitarium, February 2014. I live close to Waverly. There is a house in this location today.

The Stoddard Johnston Building, which used to be the U of L daycare in the 1980s and '90s.

PART THREE

WELCOME TO ADULTHOOD

CHAPTER 14

THREE WEDDINGS...

I graduated from the University of Louisville once again in 2011, this time with a Master of Arts in Communication. The ceremony was held downtown at the newly opened KFC Yum Center. I spent so much time focusing on grad school that I didn't give much thought about what I was going to do after graduation, at least not until the final semester. At some point during the two years in grad school, I realized the program wasn't preparing me for any sort of job. U of L's program was more theoretical in nature, intended to be a stop in the road in the journey toward a PhD.

I had a decent amount of money saved up and no student loan debt, so I could afford to take some time to consider my next move. I narrowed down my PhD program choices to Purdue, the University of Kentucky, and South Florida. Purdue and UK were the closest notable Communication PhD programs. USF seemed an interesting idea, with the program being more qualitative in nature. I thought qualitative methods were my strength even though my advisor Dr. Janet Gregory felt otherwise. I almost failed the qualitative comprehensive exit exam because I rented the textbook the previous semester and didn't have any access to it for the test. Thus, I was back to applying to yet more schools, paying more application fees, and writing more essays.

Almost as if right on schedule, disaster struck. In early June, right as I finished my Purdue essay, the phone rang. It was a panicked call from Eric.

"Mom...Mom fell again today. She was shopping at K-Mart. She was wheeling her shopping cart to the car and fell. She is at the hospital right now."

"Hang on, I'll be over in a few minutes and we'll figure things out from there," I replied. My initial instinct figured something had gone wrong with the cart or that something odd had occurred beyond a typical fall.

Eric and I went to the hospital to see what was going on. The doctor had a troubling prognosis. "Your mother completely shattered her elbow when she fell. There's nothing we can do with it as is, so we'll have to do surgery and implant a plastic replacement elbow. With practice, she should have a decent amount of use in her right arm."

I wish I could say this news shocked me, but it didn't. My mom, Phyllis, had been increasingly prone to falls, her multiple sclerosis becoming worse with time. Eric, my girlfriend, Amanda McClung, and I visited my dad in the nursing home to tell him about what had happened. He didn't seem shocked by the news either. "Honestly, your mother belongs in this place as much as I do."

My mom took a few days to heal from the surgery, but by the end of June she was back at home with the new elbow in place. She was also now in a wheelchair, so as to not risk any further falls.

In the midst of all the renewed drama, my friend Isaac was marrying his longtime girlfriend, Kate, after several years of living together. I always thought Isaac wasn't keen on getting married again given how his first marriage went, but he could only stay one step ahead of the posse for so long. Of course, Isaac had to plan the groomsmen rehearsal on a Sunday evening, July 17, the same day as the WWE *Money in the Bank* PPV. This might sound silly, but if there was ever one PPV I didn't want to miss, it was that one. CM Punk's infamous "Pipe Bomb" promo led to the main event against John Cena and had fans highly interested in the PPV. I think even Isaac wished he had come up with another time.

"Isaac, you ever get approved for disability due to your epileptic fits?" I asked.

"Not yet, but I just applied recently. Recently I had one seizure, and when I came to, I thought the year was 2003."

"2003? What a horrible thing to happen," I replied. Isaac wasn't approved for disability until 2018. Gotta love all the bureaucratic red tape.

The wedding was to be held the next evening, July 18, also my mom's birthday. An unfortunate piece of timing, but I didn't put up much of a fuss. The ceremony was at McNeeley Lake in southern Jefferson County. They were going to be married at the gazebo area in the park, which also had a nice view of the lake. Chad Black and I were among the groomsmen, with Chad being tapped for best man. The rehearsal itself was mundane, but I needed to see this thing unfold.

Sure enough, the next day Kate was late for her own wedding. Chad appeared with his fiancée, Harley, who seemed bewildered at the entire affair. I attended with Amanda and Eric. The presiding minister was a friend of Isaac's, an odd duck who was a minister of his own religion. In lieu of a typical Bible, the ceremony was to be performed using the *Book of Marvel First Appearances*, to which Harley said, "I've got to see this shit." For our part, Chad and I passed the time discussing whether the Bush tax cuts should be renewed until I said, "Amanda, if you were this late I would have long since gone home. Should I see if Isaac still wants to go through with this?"

Amanda got in Harley's car along with Megan, Isaac's nine-year-old daughter from his previous marriage. They cranked up the AC on that ninety-degree July day. Eventually, Kate and her various bridesmaids arrived, about a half hour late.

"Sorry to take so long!" she exclaimed. "My dress took forever to get ready, and I needed to bring everyone here."

From there, the wedding went off without a hitch. Unfortunately, we never heard a reading from the Marvel first appearances book since we were already running late. I wanted to hear "Love Be a Vulture Tonight," which Stan Lee riffed on in the movie *Mallrats*, but I don't think it is a real comic issue. Or maybe a solid Magneto speech from an *X-Men* issue. Alas, we didn't hear any of those, but after the ceremony, one of the bridesmaids picked up the microphone and launched into an impromptu rendition of "Amazing Grace."

From there we headed over to the now defunct Bluegrass Games on the Outer Loop for the wedding reception. Bluegrass Games was a place where Magic the Gathering tournaments were held, along with Pokémon and Dungeons & Dragons. We helped ourselves to cake and punch. I've always considered myself an enormous geek, but I would not even consider getting married using a Marvel comic and then having the reception be at a place where I played Magic the Gathering. Truly, Isaac was in a league of his own in the pantheon of geekdom.

I still needed something to do to make money until I heard from these PhD programs. An interview with Radio Shack went nowhere, so I asked Amanda what I needed to do to be a substitute teacher at Jefferson County Public Schools. (Amanda taught computer class at Rutherford Elementary before it morphed into STEM). "Believe me, they always need subs," she said in her usual twangy way, while pointing me in the direction of the online application. All you needed was sixty-four college credit hours and I obviously more than had that. I figured the process would take a few weeks until they approved my application, but in reality, it dragged on and on until nearly Christmas.

There still was the matter of K-Mart to deal with, and Chad recommended a law firm he knew willing to take the case, though I have to admit I felt lukewarm on how it was handled. I even went over to the now defunct K-Mart on the Outer Loop and scouted the parking lot. The setup was bizarre, with the handicap space my mom parked in being nowhere near the entrance and no cut-out area for a cart other than the main entrance. There was nothing but a curb the rest of the way, with speed bumps in the road to prevent easy access to other handicap spaces. I compared K-Mart's lot to other stores like Walmart or Target and none of them had a parking lot so inconvenient for the handicapped. That alone was damning enough in court, since the way the lot was set up led to her attempting to navigate the cart off the curb. I pushed a cart off the curb at K-Mart with no problems, but then again, I didn't have MS.

I called an insurance adjuster from K-Mart named Bob and had a phone conversation with him. The conversation left me in disbelief, though I shouldn't have been surprised.

"My mom fell and shattered her elbow at one of your stores. What are you prepared to do?" I asked.

"I talked to your mother after the fall," he replied. "She said there was nothing wrong with the cart itself, and I have pictures of the parking lot in front of me and I see nothing out of the ordinary."

"You talked to my mom when she was in the hospital high on morphine. She had no idea what she was saying. I have no idea whether the cart was faulty or not, but the parking lot itself is so poorly designed it led to her fall."

"As far as we're concerned, K-Mart isn't at fault here."

"See you in court then, asshole."

There was one major problem with my mom's replacement elbow: It didn't work. In fact, within a few weeks her right arm was so infected with MRSA that she had to go back to the hospital. The doctor informed Eric and me the replacement elbow wasn't a good idea and wasn't going to work. The doctor made the decision to remove the plastic replacement, leaving my mom without any particular use of her right arm.

Making matters worse, while she was back in the hospital with the MRSA, she also had yet another fall and broke her hip. I asked her what happened when Eric and I visited. "I needed to go to the bathroom badly and I rang and rang for a nurse for a solid hour, but no one ever came. I got up out of bed and went to the bathroom myself. I made it there well enough but fell on the way back."

This latest injury pushed back her recovery a few months. In fact, to this day she still has a metal rod inserted in her hip and leg from the fall. Needless to say, I asked my mom's attorney whether the hospital should also become part of the lawsuit, but for whatever reason he declined to go in that direction. Even though I felt the nurses were negligent, I suppose the argument would have been Mom shouldn't have attempted to go to the bathroom alone regardless. This development might also hurt the main K-Mart case, since it made her seem prone to falling (which was sadly becoming true).

All of this turmoil took a terrible mental toll on Eric. While I had my own apartment, a girlfriend, and possible PhD programs to look forward to, Eric had *nothing* to look forward to. He had been around my dad being at home in a wheelchair since he was seven years old, and now he was looking at a future of having to deal with my mom being in a wheelchair as well. Eric had barely managed to graduate from Valley High School in 2009, after having to repeat his senior year. Right after he graduated, everything started cratering between my mom and dad, and he was in the middle of the turmoil.

During the summer and fall of 2011, I would often go over to my mom's house and find Eric staring at the wall. Or maybe he would wash his hands and take five minutes as he stood there silently. I tried to cheer him up by having a festival of all the spaghetti westerns I could find. I don't mean only the Sergio Leone "Man with No Name" movies, but anything from the genre that sounded interesting at all. Anything in the Top 20 on spaghetti-western.net. Of course, *The Great Silence* didn't help his mindset, as it is the single most downbeat spaghetti western of them all and depressed him further. I subjected Amanda to most of these movies as well, and even to this day she shudders when I mention anything about watching another spaghetti western.

In addition to all of this turmoil, another life-changing bombshell occurred: Amanda was pregnant. The amusing aspect was that she didn't even tell me. I was the one who asked her, and after a point insisted she try a couple of home pregnancy tests, which came back positive. She exercised caution about this situation. "I mean, if I *was* pregnant, what happens then?"

"Then I guess we would have a baby," I said.

I met Amanda on the now defunct Louisville Mojo website in July 2004, which had quite a few personal ads. There were several deranged females on the site, the kind that sent you messages like "Hey, I chipped my tooth in a bar fight last night. Wanna meet?"

Imagine my surprise at finding a cute honey blonde girl who simply said, "I just finished my degree at Spalding, and I live with my grandma." Coincidentally, she lived in Prairie Village right around the corner from my mom's house.

She was out of town in Ft. Myers when I first emailed, but once she returned, we agreed to meet up at Prairie Village's ballpark behind Stonestreet Elementary. In fact, we first met on July 18, my mom's birthday. We talked for a while, barely even making eye contact, before going back to her grandma's house where I read a couple of her short stories from school. After a while I needed to leave, since my family was going to watch *Bad Boys 2* for my mom's birthday. She gave me a hug on the way out.

The first thing I noticed about Amanda was her prosthetic leg and scoliosis, which she hadn't mentioned in any of the emails. In recent years I have mentioned to her if she had revealed this info early on, I wouldn't have bothered meeting her and that would have been a major mistake. The first time Amanda came over to my mom's house, my dad asked if she had played softball at PRP, to which she later said, "That was kinda weird since I have one good leg."

Our first date was to see *The Village*, which I joked later, "Be glad we had a second date after seeing that movie." We saw many movies back then, including *The Manchurian Candidate* remake, which we saw the last weekend the old Showcase Cinemas on Bardstown Road was open. Amanda didn't quite understand why the theater closing meant so much to me, so I called Chad. The last day the Showcase was open, Chad and I saw Jet Li in *Hero* to properly end an era.

Back then, Amanda always told me, "You don't need to tell me you love me unless you mean it."

Eventually I told her "I love you," and I meant it, but I wasn't sure how much I meant it.

As time went on, Amanda expected me to go to Valley View Church with her and her grandma on Sundays, but over time I became more and more disillusioned with what I perceived as the preacher using thinly-veiled political commentary to sway people into his own conservative views. Eventually, I got fed up and quit going. This, combined with Amanda's hesitancy to be intimate, led me to break things off with her around Thanksgiving 2004. I still remember her breaking down in tears in my car on what was supposed to be the last time we saw each other. Oddly enough, we went to eat at Tumbleweed the next day, our breakup off to a rousing start.

A funny thing happened, though. Amanda didn't let me go back into my typical isolation. She always sent me an IM or email discussing her own sub jobs in the days before she taught at JCPS full time. By early 2005, we were more or less back together after she invited me to come with her and her grandma to the Old Spaghetti Factory. What else was I going to do? I didn't have this massive line of females waiting to go out with me at that point, or any other point.

Even then, I always kept Amanda at arm's length. We might see each other at my mom's house on Wednesday nights after Amanda went to church, on Fridays where we would eat at the now defunct Golden Wall not far from my apartment, and maybe spend some time together on Sundays. This was our routine for several years, but I always had one foot out the door. Given I was desperate to start film school and leave town, I didn't fully committed to anything with Amanda for several years. In fact, we had only spent two nights together in the seven years we had known each other. One time when her grandma was in the hospital in November 2008, when Amanda spent the night at my apartment after we saw *Role Models*. The other was Super Bowl weekend in 2009 when a freak ice storm hit Louisville and knocked out power in Prairie Village, though in that case Eric also spent the night at my apartment.

For whatever reason, once I turned thirty and went back to U of L for my master's, Amanda became okay with full-on sex, though she never bothered with birth control pills. I've never asked why she had a change of heart, but given her physical handicap, I felt the need to figure out if we could even have a high-quality love life before worrying about marriage. That same summer, I showed Amanda a Wheeler & Woolsey movie for the first time (*Hips, Hips, Hooray*), and when she very much enjoyed it, I let out a sigh of relief. Maybe she really was the girl for me. Once my dad went into the nursing home in early 2010, Amanda came over to my mom's house more often. I even helped her look for a new car in August 2010, the Hyundai Elantra she has to this very day.

In 2010, Amanda penned a letter and gave it to me before leaving my apartment one day, saying in effect, "We've been going together for quite a while now and I need to know what we're doing here. You are my love." There had been a few girls I'd been interested in over the years, and most of them had broken my heart in one way or another. Amanda was the only one who never did, the only one who was always there. The only one willing to put up with my prickly demeanor. I've never entirely understood why. In a way I think that's a big part of what life is all about, finding one person willing to put up with all your crap. But even then, I was still trying to get away from Louisville.

The first person we broke the pregnancy news to was my brother. "Eric, what do you think of becoming an uncle? Because that's what is going to happen."

He was stunned for a moment, but then responded, "Wow. I mean, yeah, that's great."

"We are trying to figure out potential baby names. It's going to be a boy."

"Call him Paco," Eric replied, semi-seriously. "We've seen about a hundred spaghetti westerns lately and there is a bandit named Paco in all of them."

The next day I went to visit my mom at Essex Nursing Home and Rehab Center, where she was rehabbing her hip and arm. I broke the news about Amanda's pregnancy and my mom briefly put her head down, then had a slight smile before saying, "Oh my." I even mentioned Eric's silly Paco name idea, then my own goofy idea of "Rowger," Amanda's silly nickname for me. "I guess he could be Rowger Paco," my mom jested. My silly pet name for Amanda was "Boof," in the days before Brett Kavanaugh's confirmation hearing gave Boof a more questionable meaning. Soon after, we also broke this news to my dad, around the time of the 2011 World Series.

"You see what Pujols did to the Rangers the other night?" he asked.

"Yeah, but the Rangers are now up 3–2 in the series. Oh, and Amanda is also pregnant."

Without batting an eye, my dad replied, "I think it's time for you all to get married."

"I agree," I replied.

I had no idea what sort of ring to buy or even what ring I could afford, given I was unemployed and waiting to hear from JCPS about my substitute application. I had an interview with Humana, which went nowhere. The interview coincided with Amanda finding out the sex of the baby, so I was very distracted. Amanda sent me a link to a solid-looking, affordable ring on the Shane Company website, so I used my credit card and bought it. The ring was delivered to my apartment on Thursday, October 27, also the day of the famous Game 6 of the World Series.

I went over to my mom's house that night to watch a combination of the game as well as our usual TNA Impact viewing. I switched back and forth while Eric and I drank a couple of beers, but figured the game was all but over after Texas plated three runs in the seventh inning. After watching the end of TNA, I turned to Eric and said, "Well, should we watch the end of the game?" That was when we saw the insanity unfold in the bottom of the ninth, as the Rangers were one strike away from winning the World Series, only to have the Cardinals fight back as David Freese hit a game-tying triple to right field.

That game was insane. It went into extra innings, as Josh Hamilton hit a two-run homer in the 10th, but the Cardinals scored two runs in their half of the tenth to tie it, once more being one strike away from defeat. In the bottom of the 11th, Freese came to the plate yet again.

"What would you do if he parked one right now?" I asked Eric. Sure enough, that was exactly what Freese did, and the Cardinals won the single greatest baseball game I had ever seen, 10–9. We were both in disbelief at the game.

I spent the next day reliving this amazing game. Even though the Louisville Bats are the AAA affiliate for the Cincinnati Reds, I've long since been more of a fan of the Cardinals. In the '80s and '90s, Louisville was the home of the Cardinals' AAA team, the Redbirds. The drive from Tanglewood to the fairgrounds to see the Redbirds at the now demolished Cardinal Stadium was easy, but in the late '90s the team's affiliations switched (briefly to Milwaukee, then Cincy). Today, the Louisville Bats play downtown at Slugger Field. Chad was of course a huge Cardinals fan since his dad lived in St. Louis.

That evening, right before Game 7 of the World Series, was when I planned to pop the question officially. The moment was hardly suspenseful since Amanda practically picked the ring and was busy figuring out a wedding site. While Eric was in the shower, I took Amanda back to the bedroom, got down on one knee, and pulled out the ring.

"Will you marry me?" I asked.

"Well, yeah," she responded.

"Um, here is the Shane Company warranty info, you might want to take a look at some point," I said in oh-so-romantic fashion. The proposal may not sound terribly romantic, and frankly to Amanda it probably wasn't, but to me it was one of the most romantic moments of my life. At least I didn't make Amanda take a U of L version of Steve Guttenberg's 200 question sports test from the movie *Diner*. For the record, the Cardinals went on to win Game 7 with the score of 6–2, and thus won the World Series.

Given my mom's health concerns, Eric and I looked into our options in order to protect assets if she had to go to a nursing home full time at some point in the future. Once she left Essex in November, we contacted another lawyer in order to do a nominal transfer of the house into Eric's name, with me as a minority owner as well. In the end, Eric got 75% of the house, I took 25%. I didn't want more. It wasn't my home. I was told that years ago.

Overall, 2011 was an earth-shaking year. Since graduating with my master's in May, I had dealt with my mom's injury, Eric's strange behavior, and Amanda's pregnancy. One of these events alone was enough, but all of them hit in the span of a few months. I was finally dragged kicking and screaming into adulthood.

CHAPTER 15

...AND A PACO

Since Amanda was still teaching up until the winter break, the wedding was planned for December 17 at a place in Old Louisville called Inn at the Park. It was an old Victorian-style mansion overlooking Central Park. The guy who ran the place, Herb, also performed the wedding ceremonies in the main house. My mom was back home by this point, but the Inn wasn't accessible for someone in a wheelchair, so she stayed home. With my dad also in the nursing home, Eric was my lone family member at the wedding.

Chad acted as best man, with Harley there to help Amanda prepare for the ceremony. Amanda's maid of honor was Teresa Hartley, someone she took graduate-level classes with who also taught in Jefferson County Public Schools. Isaac and Kate were also in attendance. I gave Isaac and Chad each a copy of *The Great Silence* for being groomsmen. Isaac later remarked how shocked he was by the ending of the film. I'm not sure if Chad ever watched it or not.

The ceremony itself was understated and charming, performed in the living room area of the main house near a Christmas tree. I met some of Amanda's family who I had never seen before, people from the Clarkson area such as her Native American stepfather, Tom. Chad and

Harley didn't linger very long after the ceremony since Chad had tickets for the U of L/Memphis basketball game at the KFC Yum Center.

The original plan called for us to eat at Old Spaghetti Factory that evening, but with the game at the KFC Yum Center, OSF was so packed we couldn't get in. We went to the bar next door instead and ate some fish and chips and watched the last part of the game. U of L won 95–87. I turned to Amanda and said, "Be glad U of L won that game. There's no way I was putting up with losing to Memphis on our wedding day. It couldn't happen."

We stayed in the Ambassador Suite and not the Bridal Suite, for reasons that escape me. The labyrinthine room was confusing to navigate, with a long hallway leading to a back bathroom with a jacuzzi tub. Obviously, the usual honeymoon activities applied that night, but we also found time to snuggle in the bed and watch parts of *Frosty the Snowman* on TV.

Our honeymoon featured a quick trip to Indianapolis and not much else. We left a week before Christmas, so we didn't have time for anything too epic. Instead, I bought a couple of tickets to see the horrible, winless Indianapolis Colts in the painful year when Peyton Manning had a neck injury and missed the entire season. (Manning left for Denver the following year.) For whatever reason, our honeymoon good luck rubbed off on the dreadful Colts as they picked up their first win of the season against the Tennessee Titans 27–13.

Other highlights included seeing *Mission Impossible: Ghost Protocol* at the IMAX theater at the State Museum, as well as seeing *Sherlock Holmes: A Game of Shadows* at the Circle Centre Mall before also doing some downtown shopping. We managed to find the Indianapolis Old Spaghetti Factory and ate there since we were denied it on our wedding night. Once we returned, the next couple of days involved applying for our official marriage license, as well as Amanda going to the Social Security office to have her name officially changed to Paige. After years of having students mispronounce McClung as Miss Lungs and who knows what else, she was quite glad to now be

Paige. Amanda also packed up some of her things and moved into my apartment.

I received the letter from JCPS right before Christmas and called to set up a substitute orientation. I started subbing when school resumed in January. The first school I subbed at was Rutherford, Amanda's school (which isn't far from Beechmont). I picked an easy day doing ESL. My eyes opened drastically, though, as I subbed the rest of the school year. I quickly realized elementary was not for me, as I had nightmarish days at Gutermuth, Rutherford (trying library), Luhr, Blue Lick, and several other schools. I couldn't believe how awful behavior had gotten in JCPS and quickly pivoted to subbing at the better high schools in the county. I wanted as much Manual as I could find on the sub site, since Manual is the best school in Kentucky. Male was also good, ditto my old school Butler for a while, though as I would come to realize, Butler was in the process of a serious decline that continues to this day.

The first time I went back to sub at Butler was amusing, as I tried to find out if any of the same teachers were still there. Sure enough, Mr. Hensley was still there. I had him for Physics junior year. Mr. Campbell, my old typing teacher, was still around. But most notably, Mrs. Gutermuth was still there and during planning I made sure to talk to her. I told her I had recently gotten married, Amanda was expecting, and she remembered me. She even remembered me writing my script *Welcome to Paradise* during her class. I even confessed at long-last that I never read a single page of *The Dollmaker*. She replied, "Given the kids now, I couldn't even teach a book like *The Dollmaker*."

"Did you even teach it back then?" I asked jokingly.

Everything was a waiting game until the baby arrived. Amanda and I decided on a serious name, Andrew Ryan, a semi-flip of my first and middle names, and not the absurd Paco name Eric wanted (though Isaac still calls Andrew "Paco" to this day). Another waiting game involved finding out about my PhD applications from the University of Kentucky, Purdue, and the University of Southern Florida. I was hoping for three rejection letters so I could move on to something else.

Sure enough, UK and Purdue sent those rejection letters by early March.

However, things became a whole lot more complicated when the letter and email arrived from USF. I was accepted into the Communication PhD program with a full graduate teaching assistantship for the Fall 2012 semester. They bought into my essay about being enthralled with qualitative methods. I was initially thrilled to hear this news, but then the reality hit of wondering how moving to Tampa would work.

In the midst of pending fatherhood and a potential move to Tampa, another wedding was upcoming as well. Chad and Harley were getting married on April 14. Before that, Chad planned a bachelor party at Diamond's Pub, a sports bar in the Highlands, which happened to take place on March 24. Being Chad, he planned to head to a strip club afterward, but I declined the invite. Oddly, Harley was quite accepting of this and even wanted to go on the strip club odyssey, but this was a guys' night out.

The timing couldn't have been better since U of L was in the midst of a surprising run to the Elite 8 vs. Florida. The Gators jumped out to a 40–27 halftime lead, which had the entire party dejected and quiet, but I mentioned to Chad, "There is no way they can keep shooting that well in the second half." Sure enough, U of L managed to rally and took the lead late in the game. After Wayne Blackshear made one last free throw for the Cards to go up 72–68, the entire room burst out in celebration as U of L was headed to the Final 4. High fives and hugs abounded, and all was right in the world. I was on cloud nine as I drove back to my mom's house, and upon entering the house started the chant, "C! A! R! D! S!" U of L would go on to lose to UK in the Final 4 the following week.

The mention of a strip joint odyssey sounds like the same old Chad, but in reality, he had cleaned up his act from his 2005–07 nadir. After a life-threatening aneurysm in mid-2007, doctors informed Chad's mom that he had drugs in his system at the time. This led to a reckoning. Chad straightened himself out and finished his political science degree at U of L. Similar to me, Chad had attempted at various times to leave Louisville only to be dragged back. He initially left before my senior year of high school in 1996 (after an argument with his mom's boyfriend), living with his dad in St. Louis for most of the 1996–97 school year.

In late 2000, he up and moved to Clearwater, Florida, one weekend and spent the next year working for Budweiser and living on the beach. Both times he came back, likely in part due to having a handicapped brother. I've never asked Chad how he and Harley met, mainly because he lived way out in the east end by this point and I saw less of him.

Completing the wedding trifecta, Chad and Harley were married that Saturday in April. Amanda was due in a little over a week, so Chad didn't ask either of us to be involved in the wedding itself. Isaac and I were invited, but not as groomsmen. The wedding itself took place in a large banquet hall at U of L's Shelby Campus. Isaac, Kate, Amanda, and I sat at the same table.

"So, who is the best man, you or me?" Isaac asked.

"It's not me. I had nothing to do with this wedding," I responded. The best man was another of Chad's friends, Jeff Holmes. I knew Jeff a little but wasn't especially friendly with him. I always thought Jeff's family came from money, though, so his selection as best man over Isaac or me fit Chad's east-end upward mobility motif. I also ran into Chad's dad, and we reminisced about the time I visited his house in St. Louis in late 2007 and we went to the Rams/Packers game where Brett Favre broke the all-time passing record. We followed that with a St. Louis Blues hockey game.

Following the wedding itself, Chad and Harley embarked on a major European honeymoon, going to both London and Paris. Maybe Europe wasn't Indianapolis in December or Bluegrass Games, but it would do.

Friday night, April 20. Life changed once and for all. Amanda had finished her last school day of the year before maternity leave. Amanda and I were watching old episodes of *CSI: Miami* on TV when Amanda got up to go to the bathroom. All of a sudden, a sizable amount of liquid plopped out of her and hit the floor. She already had an appointment for a C-section scheduled for Tuesday, but her water had broken. Strangely enough, neither of us particularly freaked. We threw a few things together and headed out to Suburban Hospital.

Amanda's contractions became more frequent by the time we got to a prep room, but given her scoliosis, a typical birth was out of the question. She had to have a C-section. She kept repeating "Oh, get this kid out of me!" as the nurses readied her. Everything was ready in the delivery room, and Amanda was wheeled in. They didn't allow me to go in, so instead I waited in a chair outside the room. I could hear some occasional talk about an epidural as the doctor tried inserting the huge needle into Amanda's back, but again, the scoliosis made it impossible. As they kept attempting the epidural, I heard Amanda screaming in agony until she finally yelled, "Put me to sleep and get this kid out of me!" Soon after, the screaming stopped. They put her to sleep.

A few minutes later, I heard a baby crying, so I assumed everything was going according to plan. A nurse exited the delivery room and casually said, "You can go in now." I rushed into the room and the place was a scene out of a *Saw* movie, with blood and guts everywhere. Amanda was still unconscious, and they had covered her up. I walked to the other side of the room and saw the newborn. Andrew Ryan Paige was born at 2:48 a.m. on April 21, 2012. He weighed six pounds, twelve ounces. I took a quick picture on my phone to document the occasion. I didn't take other pictures of the delivery room, lest they be mistaken for crime scene photos.

A few minutes later, I joined Amanda in the recovery room. We were the only ones there that late at night, and the basement room had an isolated and slightly spooky vibe. Eventually a nurse wheeled Andrew in and let me hold him. I had no idea how to hold a newborn, but he had calmed down by this point and mostly sucked his thumb. Amanda, for her part, had a yellowish hue and was barely conscious. While holding Andrew, I turned to Amanda and said, "So, are you ready for number two?" She responded with a pitiful whimper. I sat there with Amanda, holding Andrew, for what seemed like an eternity until the nurse came back to take him. Since Amanda was still a living corpse, I decided to go back to the apartment. I tried to crash, but never could.

With no further complications, Amanda and Andrew both came home on Tuesday, the day the original C-section was scheduled. The first night with Andrew was exhausting, as he cried through the night. After a while we got into a decent pattern of feedings and diaper changes and about three months later he was able to sleep through the night.

Unfortunately, Andrew came home to an apartment that had quickly turned into a disaster. A couple of months earlier, I had noticed a few bugs crawling around on the couch and easy chair over at my mom's house. This was a case of bed bugs. Since we spent a considerable amount of time there, the bed bugs spread to the apartment as well. I'm still not sure where they came from but given my mom's various hospital and nursing home stays, I'd say one of those is a decent bet, though she insists I brought them back from a debate tourney. We often woke up with red spots from the bed bug bites. Tanglewood charged me $200 to send someone up to spray, half of my original deposit.

Even more inexcusable, the apartment now had an infestation of mice as well. I first recall seeing something dark scurry across the floor during the UK/Kansas NCAA title game, and after a point we could hear a mouse rummaging through potato chip bags in the kitchen. I even occasionally saw one jump between gas openings on the stove. They got in through the balcony door since the maintenance crew at the complex had screwed up the wood underneath the door while replacing planks. There was now a slight opening between the wood and the door where mice could slip through. I still had no idea where they came from, though, since we were on the second floor.

Making matters even worse, the ceiling in the bedroom was starting to collapse, with a bad storm being the initial cause. A maintenance man had to hammer a piece of wood up there to keep the ceiling from falling any further. Sometimes late at night I could hear mice scratching at the area, trying to claw their way in.

I tried sticky traps that spring/summer and caught a couple of mice. I even tried actual mouse traps and could hear them snap from another room as the trap practically tore a mouse in two. Eventually they figured out the traps. Once while Amanda and I were watching TV with Andrew asleep, one mouse snuck up to the trap by the balcony door, carefully ate some of the cheese without tripping the trap, stared at us with piercing black eyes, and then left under the door. I turned to Amanda and said, "We have to move." Tanglewood wasn't renewing the lease, anyway. Three people was one too many for a one-bedroom apartment. We needed to either rent a two-bedroom apartment or find somewhere else. I think we wanted to go anywhere else.

Further complicating matters, Amanda started having severe stomach pain in late May. We called EMS and she was taken back to Suburban Hospital where the doctors realized Amanda needed her gallbladder removed. The surgery didn't happen immediately but was scheduled for a couple of weeks later. I still tried to sub a few days at the end of the school year, but otherwise needed to stay home with Andrew. Amanda had her gallbladder successfully removed, but her digestive system was screwy for quite a while after the surgery. My mom and Eric helped look after Andrew while Amanda was laid up in the hospital on and off in May and June. I took all of this in stride. I mostly quit drinking beer. I felt more focused now that we were married, and I had a partner in life.

There was also the matter of USF, which had become quite the elephant in the room. Given my mom's health problems and the ongoing lawsuit against K-Mart, as well as having a newborn baby at home, I didn't see any feasible way I could move all the way to Tampa. One day at my mom's house, I read off the course descriptions of the classes I would be taking and I didn't even understand half of what they were talking about. Going to USF for PhD studies was a nice goal, but I could live without a doctorate. With some regret, in May I informed the USF communication department I wasn't going to be able to attend due to my new commitments. They understood and even mentioned delaying my entrance for a year, but I never heard anything else about it. With that decision, the idea of leaving Louisville faded into memory.

We had until the end of summer break to find a new home. Amanda and I looked at a few different condos and patio-style homes, as well as one house not too far from my mom's in Prairie Village. None of them stood out. We toured a patio home with a proverbial white picket fence in a community nestled right in back of Waverly Hills Sanitarium. For whatever reason, perhaps because it was a model home and we saw what it looked like with furniture, the house clicked. We informed real estate agent Judd Biggs we would take it, and the buying process started. The developer went bankrupt during the 2008 real estate crash, so the price was cheaper than normal provided we sign a bizarre ten-year mortgage (which Chad later helped us refinance in late 2019).

During the summer, Amanda's Grandma Mary had a serious stroke that left her unable to speak. The timing was strange, her falling ill and having to go to Essex Nursing Home a few months after Amanda moved out. We didn't deal with Mary's situation, though, since Amanda's aunt Patty had the power of attorney and was responsible for selling the house on Silverwood. We occasionally visited her from time to time, and Amanda brought Andrew so her grandma could see him.

By mid-August, the closing was finalized. I spent another $200 to break the lease at Tanglewood, so now my initial deposit of $409.50 was gone and I never saw it again. Amanda hired Two Men and a Truck to help us move, and in the process of heaving everything, one of the wooden planks on the staircase broke and became dangerous to navigate as we carried everything out of the apartment once and for all. Tanglewood refused to let me leave. I had lived all of my thirty-three years at Tanglewood, either at #304, #306, or #607 Bermuda Lane. Once I turned in the door keys to the office and left Tanglewood for the last time, I never looked back. Once we settled into our new house, I realized for the first time in my life I had an actual home.

My mom's K-Mart lawsuit dragged on until early 2013, when K-

Mart proposed a settlement that would net my mom $80,000. I didn't want her to accept those terms, but the attorney wasn't sold on the case and felt K-Mart's lawyers would go after my mom as being an accident-prone older woman with MS.

"Tell them we'll see them in court. I'm sure the jury will love a soulless corporation going after a woman with one good arm sitting in a wheelchair," I responded.

By this point, my mom wanted the whole thing to go away, so she accepted the offer. Eighty grand for a permanent injury? As far as I'm concerned, K-Mart got off cheap. That particular store didn't stay in business much longer, anyway, going under and sitting vacant until a Peddler's Mall moved in a few years later. At the end of the day, my mom is still here, and K-Mart isn't, so maybe there is some justice in this world. Eric, for his part, took her to Southwest Hospital for most of 2012 to receive IV meds to keep the MRSA out of her injured arm.

The bed bugs followed us from the apartment to the new house, like a horror movie villain showing up in the last scene for a final scare. They were also a persistent problem for my mom until she called an exterminator. We finally got rid of them once and for all after calling Okolona Pest Control, who turned up the heat in the house to about 120 degrees.

Given U of L's sports success over the next year, I felt rewarded for staying in town. U of L pulled a shocking upset of Florida in the Sugar Bowl, 33–23. And of course, in 2013 the Cardinals won the big one in basketball for the first time since 1986, defeating Michigan in the championship game, 82–76. Eric and I went to Lucas Oil Stadium in Indianapolis for the Duke Elite 8 game and saw the single greatest second half in the history of U of L basketball as the Cards destroyed the Blue Devils, 85–63. Ironically, I went to the bathroom at the under 8:00 timeout in the first half and missed the infamous Kevin Ware broken leg moment, returning to find a hushed silence in the stadium.

On the way back, we stopped at Ruby Tuesday in Edinburgh, Indiana, the only place open late on Easter Sunday. As we were being seated, I noticed a huge roar from the bar area where a group of U of L fans had gathered around the TVs. The U of L women had pulled a shocking upset of Brittney Griner and #1 Baylor. The Lady Cards went all the way to the title game as well but were rolled badly by UConn. For their part, Chad and Harley went to Atlanta for the Final 4, later describing it as a life-changing experience.

As I went down to sub at Manual the next day, I drove through the U of L campus. The sun was rising to reveal a beautiful spring morning. I couldn't help but reminisce about my various times at U of L daycare and also later as a student. All the various times us daycare kids played on the concrete 1980 NCAA championship memorial outside Crawford Gym (the gym was destroyed in 2016). I fought off tears, but they were tears of joy this time. After I got home, I hopped on Facebook and typed out the following message:

"I'm just putting this into some perspective. Earlier today some people ridiculed me for a half serious comment that U of L's 1986 title win was the best day of my life...and that title win happened when I was in 1st grade. Since then, I graduated elementary school, middle, HS, went to college at U of L, then after a long hiatus went back for an MA (also from U of L), got married, and had a kid. In the meantime, I watched U of L drift from contender to 'Glad to be in the Sweet 16' status for most of the 1988–94 period, came tantalizingly close to doing something special my senior year of HS only to see DeJuan Wheat get hurt in the Sweet 16 vs. Texas and the team had no magic left vs. UNC. Endured the horrific final Crum years coinciding with my undergrad years, where U of L didn't win a single NCAA tournament game.

I was stoked when U of L hired Pitino and over the past 12 years have felt the utmost joy (2005 regional final vs. WVU), damn near gone crazy over some losses (DePaul in 2003 and several vs. Marquette come to mind), even experienced the low point of U of L losing to Morehead in the tourney. But I have always kept the faith, hoping someday U of L would once again reign supreme. So yeah, as someone whose mom worked at U of L for two decades, went to U of L daycare, grew up on the campus, met the likes of Milt Wagner (who showed us daycare kids his 1986 championship ring), Pervis Ellison, and Felton Spencer at Crawford Gym, and has two degrees from U of L, I don't mind telling you this is about as good as it gets."

Nowadays I can't help but look at the disaster U of L men's basketball has become after numerous NCAA scandals, how all of those wins have been vacated, and the feeling is very bittersweet. Some of the best times of my life involved cheering on the 2012 and 2013 U of L basketball teams, and now none of those accomplishments are officially recognized.

Those years saw earth-shattering changes in my life, and I still look back on that era with a certain fondness. But there was a lot of heartache to go along with it. I became a Louisville lifer during this period. I missed the last boat off the island and now had to watch as it sailed away into the sunset, until it was out of view.

CHAPTER 16

THE KING OF CRYPTO

By the middle of 2016, I had finished my Master of Arts in Teaching from the University of the Cumberlands online program. I wanted to become a full-time social studies teacher with JCPS. There was one significant problem, however. I felt increasingly burnt out from subbing. Even though I had applied for several jobs at JCPS, I never heard about a single one of them. As such, I started looking at other avenues to make money.

I'd heard of Bitcoin as far back as 2012 but had no idea how it worked or what practical use it had. BTC appeared on my radar much more in the second half of 2016 when I saw the price of BTC had gone all the way up to $500. My first experience buying Bitcoin was on Circle.com. I wanted to buy $5.00 worth of BTC, but accidentally bought 5 BTC to the tune of $2,500 and sent it to my newly installed Electrum desktop wallet. I freaked out and called customer service and the woman from Circle told me to send it back to them for a refund, which I did. I later massively regretted doing so, since 5 BTC would now be worth six figures on a $2,500 investment.

BTC rose to $700 from $500 in the span of a week after the botched Circle purchase, total insanity. I tried to buy the same 5 BTC again using my Platinum credit card, but the charge was declined because my bank viewed it as a suspicious purchase. There were several opportunities here to make money and I blew each and every one of them.

I spent quite a few months in 2017 researching crypto coins and started seeing massive dollar signs. The returns these coins could provide could be absurd if you could get in on the ground floor of a promising project. For example, when I signed up for Coinbase, I recall Ethereum being about $11, but didn't know what ETH was yet. As of this writing, ETH is worth $1,850 and has gotten as high as $4,000. Litecoin was about $4 and is now worth $90, but at various points has been worth over $300.

Chaotic market swings have been a major problem for crypto. A coin might be worth quite a bit one day, then worthless the next. Even BTC was subject to these market swings. As such, I didn't feel good keeping my own money tied up in crypto, and things would soon get a whole lot worse. Amanda, for her part, was baffled by the idea of cryptocurrency in the first place, noting, "It's nothing. It's something someone came up with that doesn't really exist but has some random value."

As 2017 progressed, I researched some other off-the-wall, lesser-known coins. For instance, Enjin Coin (a crypto token used for gaming) was about to hit exchanges and cost about 2 cents. I needed some capital, and my mom was grateful for me helping out with her K-Mart lawsuit, so she wrote me a check for $5,000 to invest in crypto. For whatever reason, Enjin wasn't quite at the top of my list. I wasn't sold on it enough. If I had invested that $5,000 in Enjin Coin in late 2017, I could have sold it off five years later and made close to a million dollars. Hindsight is 20/20, however.

The crypto coin on my mind in late 2017 was Substratum. I heard about it on various YouTube clips, with hype men waxing poetic about Substratum. It was going to be a "game changer," or that it could "change the world," and all sorts of other flowery verbiage ascribed to countless other scam coins. Still, at the time I was quite interested, so I eagerly awaited Substratum's arrival on exchanges. The BTC I bought with the $5,000 depreciated in value during the time it was locked on Coinbase (new Chinese regulations drove the price down), so now I had to wait for BTC to bounce back before I could act.

I also started looking around for other lines of work. I considered selling real estate as far back as 2009 when I shut down my movie website. I finally took the plunge in September 2017, signing up for real estate classes on the Real Estate Express online program. I went through the various modules quickly and by October 2017, I was ready to take the exam. The test wasn't hard to pass, but the various class modules and the test had one major problem: I still had zero clue how to do anything real estate oriented. The classes assumed you already had all these clients and there are plenty of details about the legality of buying and selling real estate, but not how to find the clients in the first place. Regardless, I passed the test on the first try and within days letters poured in from various brokers.

An even bigger problem with my real estate idea: I couldn't stand the vast majority of the people I met in these interviews. The first person I talked to was a woman from Coldwell Banker and she was incredibly arrogant.

"I can see you have no idea about this, so put your license in escrow and move on," she said.

Clearly, that broker was out. I talked to a couple of guys at Schuler Bauer and Weichert and they either bored me to tears or gave me no concept of what I would be doing if I joined their brokerage.

Sophia Zandor of Zandor Realty was recommended by someone Amanda knew, so I met with her. She was the most arrogant of the lot.

"If you started here, I couldn't even put you in any serious open house. Maybe stuff no one else cared about, but that's about it," she said. The more I talked to these people, the more put off by real estate I became. They didn't even try to ingratiate themselves.

The two places I seriously considered were JP Pirtle and Red Edge Realty. The guy I talked to at Pirtle at least spelled out a plan of action with some options. Since I had no customer base, I would have done the 50/50 split deal where Pirtle would provide me with leads. I wasn't thrilled with the mandatory floor time Pirtle demanded, though. Matt Hall of Red Edge Realty was the coolest realtor I talked to. His wife taught at Holy Cross, where I did my student teaching, so I had something to discuss with him. Red Edge's percentages were terrific 80/20 splits. But the whole idea of Facebook ads and whatever Hall trained agents to do didn't make sense to me. At the end of all these meetings, I told the guy at Pirtle I might be interested but would start in January. For the time being, I put my license in escrow, just like the Coldwell Banker woman said I should have done in the first place.

During all these real estate machinations I decided to take the plunge into crypto trading, and would I ever live to regret it. Word came out Substratum would soon be listed on the now defunct crypto exchange EtherDelta. That exchange is difficult to explain to crypto neophytes. It was an Ethereum-based exchange founded by Zachary Coburn in 2017 but wasn't a true centralized exchange such as Coinbase or Binance. Conversely, it also wasn't a purely decentralized exchange like Uniswap today, where you connect a Metamask browser wallet and interact with the site without providing any Know Your Customer details. I think EtherDelta used Metamask, but at the time I didn't understand Metamask. Instead, I generated an address on Ether-Delta and had to swap the BTC into ETH in order to send crypto to the address.

But wait, there's more! Once the ETH was on EtherDelta, you had to transfer it to the trading wallet on the site, which had an ETH gas fee with each transaction. (Ethereum's network runs on gas fees, which have gotten ridiculous over the years.) I messed with the site incessantly to deposit ETH onto the wallet to do any trading. It was an enormous hassle, the format being worse than any other exchange I've seen. Also, unlike a true decentralized exchange, EtherDelta had an order book similar to a typical exchange. EtherDelta existed in this hazy gray area between legit exchanges with vetted coins and purely decentralized exchanges where anyone can list whatever shitcoin they want and create a pool. At the time, I thought EtherDelta was totally legit in terms of the listings, even if the site design proved confusing.

Once I was ready to buy it, I had second thoughts about Substratum. The coin was initially listed at ten cents in the ICO (Initial Coin Offering), but on EtherDelta it had already tanked to about five cents. Feeling ominous about the future of Substratum, I backed off and didn't touch it. What's frustrating is that in the long run I was right about Substratum being useless, but there existed a brief window where it pumped up in January 2018 and reached as high as $2.60. Once again, if I had invested the money at the right moment, I could have cashed out a few months later and made about $260,000.

Instead, I decided to do something wildly stupid. I put all $5,000 worth of ETH into something called Kick Coin, another new listing on EtherDelta. This was a major mistake, since Kick Coin was a total shitcoin that turned out to be worthless within a week. A few days later I realized what a terrible mistake I had made but lost about half of the money by the time I sold it all off.

Rattled by my own mistake, I kept compounding these errors. I invested in short-term trades with one shitcoin after another and before long I had blown nearly all of the money my mom gave me screwing around on EtherDelta. As Amanda ranted, "You are really, *really* not good at this." Now chasing money, I frustratingly bought $3,000 more in ETH on Coinbase using my own money and sent it to EtherDelta. I saw a promising token on EtherDelta called eBTC, which was marketed as an Ethereum-based version of Bitcoin with the same exact coin supply. This one made perfect sense to me, so I put the three grand on it. Sure enough, eBTC was rising as I went to bed that October evening. The $3,000 had now grown to about $5,000 worth of ETH, so I figured in a few days I would recoup my losses and be profitable.

I was wrong. I woke up early the next day to sub at Manual and checked the price of eBTC. For a moment, I thought I was sleepy and not looking at the screen right. Surely a decimal was off or something. The price had cratered overnight when the developer of the coin left the project. In other words, he exit-scammed everyone. By the time I rushed to sell off the now worthless eBTC, I had about $100 left of the $3,000 I deposited.

When I told my mom about this, her reaction was oddly muted. Eric, for his part, was unbelievably pissed at me. "You blew five thousand dollars?! Are you out of your mind? My God, Mom. Why did you ever give him that money?"

"Well, I was trying to help him out. It sounded like a good idea," she replied.

"I'll get it back," I responded assuredly, almost trying to convince myself. "I just need to figure out something else."

In November 2017, I started seeing videos on YouTube of people promoting a crypto project called BitConnect. At first I was confused as to what the site entailed, and a few of these promoters seemed like complete crackpots. But a few of them made sense and explained how investing in BitConnect could generate 1–2% a day in earnings. Theoretically, BitConnect was trading BTC with an advanced level AI bot and the more volatile the BTC market, the more you earned. If the market wasn't very volatile that day, you didn't get a very good percentage.

I had nothing more to lose so I threw the last $100 on BitConnect to try the site and see how it worked. I signed up under a guy named Mason Richards, another of the promoters on YouTube who made BitConnect videos. Richards wasn't as well-known as other BitConnect promoters, but his bland, unassuming nature seemed more trustworthy than these other guys. Richards and I exchanged a few emails where he waxed poetic about the power of crypto and how much money could be made. He even recorded a video where he paid off his entire mortgage with his BitConnect earnings. It was powerful stuff. I later joined his Telegram group dedicated to BitConnect. Richards reassured me there was nothing shady about BitConnect and I wanted to believe him. After all, what idiot would put out YouTube hype videos for a total scam that could get him in trouble with the law should the scheme go belly-up?

BitConnect was a curious site to say the least, complete with their own internal exchange between BTC and the native BitConnect (BCC) coin. In order to invest, you deposited BTC on the site, swapped it to BCC, and from there made your investment. BitConnect had various platforms going all the way up to $100,010 (levels always ended in 10). In fact, I needed to buy another $10 of BTC to do the $110 initial investment. What gave me pause is once you invested money, it was locked in for a year.

Another questionable aspect of the platform was the referral system, where these various promoters convinced people to sign up under them. In retrospect, BitConnect was a classic pyramid scheme, but at the time my initial $110 generated results from a booming crypto market. I spent most of the holiday season trying to convince Amanda to do a bigger investment in BitConnect, regardless of whether we should reinvest or cash out the money until breaking even and then start the reinvests (once you earned $1,010, you could reinvest and multiply your money). I let the initial investment play out for the time being since the holidays were approaching, but I kept watching videos on BitConnect's official YouTube page.

Amanda and I went to Evansville to stay at the Tropicana Hotel for our sixth anniversary, or more specifically Le Merigot, the boutique offshoot of the Tropicana near the casino. The view of the Ohio River was slightly eerie from downtown Evansville. At that time of year, wooded debris floated furiously down the river and the banks over-flowed on the Kentucky side so you could see trees flooded by the river.

We didn't do a huge amount in Evansville. I bet on a few basketball games at the casino, as well as some of the NFL games on Sunday. We also went to see *The Last Jedi* at the AMC Theater, and I spent a couple of hours that night ranting to both Chad and Isaac about the film and its various shortcomings. We met up with my dad's old friends from Henderson, David and Lu Ann Cochran. We had dinner with them at Zuki Hibachi Grill in downtown Evansville.

I hadn't seen the Cochrans since Christmas 1994, a fact which shocked David when I told him since he had no recollection. I even remembered some of the CDs they had, such as U2's *The Joshua Tree* and Carole King's *Tapestry*. As we sat at the grill watching the food being prepared, we talked about numerous things, including my dad and his long-term health. Amanda and Lu Ann chatted between themselves, while David and I talked.

"Such a shame what happened with Danny. At the time we thought he took off and went back to Louisville. We didn't hear about his stroke until a while later," David said.

"We miss Danny, we really do," Lu Ann said.

"Why have you all not come to visit him?" I asked.

"Is he even responsive? We've been under the impression he was some kind of vegetable," David asked.

"Sure, he can talk to you and everything. He was paralyzed by the stroke, but he's hardly a vegetable. Whenever you next come to Louisville, you can see him at Clifton Oaks Nursing Home. He'd be glad to see you."

"Maybe we will. We go to Louisville for church events sometimes in Iroquois Park. You know, I always thought your grandmother's house in Henderson was a neat little house."

"Should we go see what it's like now?" I asked Amanda. She shrugged, as if to say, "Why not?"

The morning before we left for Louisville, we drove into Henderson on Highway 41. Technically you enter Kentucky about half a mile before you reach the Ohio River, which I have always found bizarre. Ellis Park, which hosts horse racing, is actually on the Indiana side of the river but is still considered Kentucky due to the baffling drawing of the original map. Once you reach Henderson, the clock may as well turn back fifteen years, with signs on the road advertising, "We will convert your VHS tapes to DVD!" and a still existing Family Video store. As we reached the corner where my paternal grandmother's house used to be, I saw nothing but a vacant lot. My dad sold the house to the owner of the Payless Shoes store next door about twenty years earlier, but Payless too was gone, replaced by a check cashing store.

"Let's go home," I told Amanda. "There's nothing to see here." My dad all but killed himself working on that house until he had a stroke, and now it didn't even exist.

On Christmas Eve, my mom got a call from Clifton Oaks. Dad was down at University of Louisville Hospital for a couple of reasons, neither of them good. From what my mom later told me, my dad convinced various nurses to let him drink Pepsi and Mountain Dew, which he was not supposed to be drinking. Thus, his blood sugar spiked similar to the way it had in 2001. Also, years of smoking had caught up to him and he now had emphysema, the same disease that killed his mother back in 1996.

We spent part of Christmas Eve down at the hospital checking on my dad to see how he was doing. My mom, Eric, and I went into the ICU while Amanda stayed with Andrew in the lobby area. Andrew was already showing signs of ADHD, so we didn't take him into the ICU area. Dad didn't seem to be in bad spirits, all in all. He was lying in bed watching a Saints/Falcons game.

"Hey, Dad, are you doing okay?" I asked.

"I'm doing okay for an old man," he replied.

"You are watching the Falcons? After the way they blew the Super Bowl, why would anyone watch them ever again?" I asked. My dad chuckled.

There wasn't much else to the visit, just a quick conversation with the doctor, who reiterated no one at the nursing home should give him sugary drinks. The doctor didn't say much about the emphysema. Once someone has it, there isn't a cure.

On the way back to the car, my mom said something that has stayed with me ever since. "Nothing...nothing kills him," she said. This was not said in a cold-blooded way, but more of a sad, heartbroken statement that really meant "Hasn't he suffered enough?" I nodded in agreement with her sentiment.

CHAPTER 17

KING OF CRYPTO: THE BITCONNECT SCAM

A couple of days after Christmas, I convinced Amanda to jump in on my BitConnect idea. She wasn't thrilled, but begrudgingly went to the bank as we wired my Gemini account $5,070. There were newfangled regulations hitting the crypto market as of January 1, 2018, so I wanted to do this transaction before those regulations took effect. On December 29, I funded a much bigger $5,010 investment on BitConnect. I still wasn't 100% sold on it, but if nothing else, we could take the first month or two and cash out the initial five grand, then have money to play around with on the platform to reinvest or do whatever we wanted.

A few days into the new year, ominous signs started showing with BitConnect. The first blow came when the Texas Securities Commission issued a cease and desist on BitConnect's operations in the state, insisting BitConnect and its promoters were selling unregistered securities. This development alarmed me, but at first there was no particular change to BitConnect's site other than not being available in Texas. About a week later, North Carolina's Secretary of State issued a cease and desist for BitConnect in that state as well. Things had become downright worrying now. The $5,010 was locked in for a year, with another $900 in daily earnings in my wallet on the site.

All hell officially broke loose over the weekend of January 13–14. I tried logging in to BitConnect, but the site was slow and not working right. Eventually the site didn't load, with a Cloudflare notice about a DDOS attack on the site. Bear in mind the BCC coin itself was worth over $300 at the beginning of the weekend, and by the end of the weekend the coin had cratered in value to about $30.

Everyone on Richards's Telegram group feared the worst, namely that those behind BitConnect were pulling one of the biggest exit scams the world had ever seen. BitConnect had been a top ten crypto on coinmarketcap.com a few weeks earlier. BitConnect released another YouTube video insisting no one had been scammed. Apparently, BitConnect had to cease operations in the United States due to increasing regulatory concerns. "In a few days, everyone will be paid off their initial amounts," the video said.

Sure enough, a couple of days later the site functioned again. The whole phony DDOS attack was a ruse designed to purposefully crash the value of the BCC coin while those behind BitConnect planned their exit. I checked my account and noticed I had been "paid" in 16.67 BCC coins, which were essentially worthless since the coin cratered in value once reality starting setting in. The BCC coins were valued at the amount of the coin before the fiasco of that weekend. I always wondered about the purpose of the BCC coin since the site was basically a BTC investment platform. Now I knew. The coin was there to pay people off in something worthless when the time came to bail.

To say I was pissed would be a gross understatement. Imagine a combination of seething anger, frustration, and even a feeling of depression. I wasn't going to take this lying down, however. The trading on EtherDelta was my own screwing up and I own up to it, but this was outright being scammed by people in amazingly brazen fashion. I looked up local attorneys that mentioned anything about cryptocurrency. Jasper Ward of Jones Ward PLC was the main name I noticed, so I called him and also sent an email. Once he responded, I sent him the info on my BitConnect deposits, all emails from Mason Richards, and anything else BitConnect related I could find.

I had a meeting with Ward and another attorney, Abigail Green, on January 25. He already had all the information from our emails, so this meeting was a formality to sign paperwork and start a lawsuit in motion. Green handled background details, and over time I found her easier to talk to than Ward.

"What I can't understand is why authorities in Texas and North Carolina issued the cease-and-desist orders," Ward pondered. "Usually for state governments to get involved, someone needs to be scammed first."

"Oh, those cease-and-desist orders are what caused the scam in the first place," I replied. "I am not an expert, so I don't know if crypto can even be considered a security, but these guys putting themselves all over YouTube doing BitConnect videos, they're insane if they were knowingly promoting a Ponzi scheme."

"Well, right now we are listing BitConnect as a defendant, as well as Mason Richards since you signed up under him. There might be a problem trying to find the people behind BitConnect itself though, since they are overseas and outside of U.S. jurisdiction. But, yeah, these people screwed a whole bunch of investors here and we are going to do our best to get your money back. Oh, and stay away from EtherDelta. That site sucks."

On January 29, Ward filed the complaint. Within the next day, Richards banned me from his Telegram group and I have had zero contact with him ever since. I had no idea if I would ever hear anything about the lawsuit again. A reporter contacted me a few days later, but Ward advised me not to speak to him. I tried to put the whole fiasco behind me. The demise of BitConnect had a jarring effect on the crypto market overall, as the price of Bitcoin cratered throughout 2018 after the insane rally in the second half of 2017. BTC started 2018 hovering around $15,000 and ended 2018 around $3,700. Crypto prices eventually bounced back, but occasionally there will be something like the FTX collapse or Terra Luna collapse to send prices reeling yet again.

Amanda's grandmother died a few months later in April. She was eighty-five and had never really recovered from her 2012 stroke, and in Amanda's words, "At least she isn't suffering anymore and is in a better place now." Amanda's aunt Patty arranged the funeral at Owen Funeral Home on Dixie. The visitation took place the day before the funeral, as a plethora of Mary's family members and people who knew her from Valley View Church all showed up to pay respects. Patty had displays of Mary's life in pictures and the song of choice was one of Mary's favorites, "I Can Only Imagine." There was even food in the large kitchen area at Owen Funeral Home. The next day, she was laid to rest at the cemetery next to Christian Assembly Church on Stonestreet Road near Dixie Highway.

By the middle of May, I became preoccupied with finishing the school year. I never joined Pirtle or Red Edge Realty, possibly because I didn't have any money now for startup expenses. I have renewed my real estate license when necessary, but it has remained in escrow ever since. Instead, I decided to keep trying for a full-time social studies job at JCPS. I finally called Human Resources and inquired about my application. I was told I needed four references instead of three, and as such my application wasn't being viewed by any schools. Three reference spots on the application had an asterisk, so anyone looking would think only three references were necessary. Sometimes these people at JCPS aren't the sharpest tools in the shed. I asked one of my college professors to write another reference, and now my application was corrected in the system.

Tuesday, May 15. I had trouble with the air conditioning in my Buick Century, so I stopped at O'Reilly's to buy some coolant. My cell phone vibrated, but I didn't answer it. Once I got home, the cell phone vibrated again, and this time I answered. It was a nurse at University of Louisville Hospital.

"Hello, we need you to come down here. We have your dad."

"How is he doing?" I asked, somewhat puzzled about this entire call.

"We just need you to come down here," she replied cryptically.

I stopped by my mom's house to pick up her and Eric. On the way down to the hospital, we speculated about what was going on and the bizarre nature of the call I received.

"I wonder if it's something serious?" my mom asked.

"I doubt it. Wouldn't the nurse have said something on the phone?" I wondered.

Once we arrived at the hospital, a nurse ushered us into a private waiting room. I had never been in such a room at a hospital. Within minutes, a doctor arrived in the room and shut the door. Very strange. Something different was going on here.

"I am here to inform you that Stanley Daniel Paige has died."

The rest of the hospital visit was a blur. I don't remember much else about the conversation with the doctor. Blood sugar again, emphysema, all his previous ailments. I was stunned, even though I shouldn't have been. I was also angry. Why didn't they say this on the phone instead of leaving the impression he was sick again? I don't remember driving my mom and Eric home, or how I got home. I texted Amanda to tell her what had happened, and we would have to talk later.

I picked up Andrew from kindergarten class at the usual time. I told him about his grandfather dying, but he didn't register anything since he had only been around my dad a few times at the nursing home. Instead, Andrew rambled on about not wanting whatever we were going to eat, going on and on until I snapped at him, "Andrew, did you not hear me? My dad died today!"

We conducted business with Owen Funeral Home on Wednesday. My dad already had a burial plan in place and Owen already had his body. My mom went over the financials of the funeral with the director, then he turned to Eric and me and said, "I need you two to find one of his suits to be buried in if you can. Also, if you have any songs your dad would have wanted played, let me know."

"He was a big Bob Seger fan," I responded. "Maybe play 'Against the Wind' first, then after the speech play 'Turn the Page.'"

"That should be easy. I have Bob Seger's *Greatest Hits* in my truck." We all chuckled.

Eric and I rummaged through the basement to find a decent suit. Eric found one horrendous looking light-and-dark-blue striped tie and jested, "This is the worst tie I have ever seen. Should we use it?" I considered it but found something more subdued. We found one of my dad's old suits and a tie and took it back to Owen Funeral Home later that day. The visitation was going to be the next evening, but we didn't contact the *Courier-Journal* about an obituary beyond whatever Owen listed. It cost a few hundred dollars, and between Amanda and me posting about the visitation and funeral on Facebook, whoever cared enough to come would get the message.

I had a previously assigned sub job the next day at Manual, and upon entering the building, the main office secretary, Bev, stopped me as I grabbed the attendance folder. "Are you working tomorrow? I have a job for you."

"Sorry, my dad died and the funeral is tomorrow."

"Oh! I'm so sorry," Bev replied.

"I should be available Monday, though, if you have anything."

I sat at the desk the entire day, hardly paying any attention to the kids. Most acted fine anyway. This was Manual, after all. I thought about my dad and the last time I spoke to him back in March when we filled out NCAA tournament brackets together. He could barely stay focused enough to fill out a bracket. I texted Chad to see if he was coming to the funeral.

"I went to my grandma's funeral recently and I don't think I can take time off again," he replied. I had never met his paternal grandmother. I would have gone if his maternal grandmother, Marnie, had died. I had been to her house a few times.

The visitation was a muted affair compared to the one for Amanda's grandmother. We didn't have much in the way of pictures for them to display, and it was only a small gathering of a few people. A couple of

Amanda's church friends popped in. Isaac and Kate also showed up and vowed to be at the funeral the next day. The director asked my mom what she wanted him to say, how she met my dad, and other questions.

"Oh, I don't know," she replied. "We met at Western when I was in college. My cousin Linda introduced us. He was the one boy who wanted anything to do with me. I guess you can say that tomorrow."

"I thought about what movies he liked," I mentioned. "He was a massive Randolph Scott fan. Maybe mention *Ride the High Country* in your speech, even though he didn't watch it as much. He practically wore out a VHS tape of *Riding Shotgun*, but I don't think that movie is as well-known."

"Hey, if it wasn't for your dad, I would have never seen a Randolph Scott movie. I would only know him as a gag in *Blazing Saddles*," Isaac jested. Isaac, the funeral director, and I all stood up and recited the Randolph Scott tribute bit from *Blazing Saddles*, complete with gasps and removing our nonexistent cowboy hats. "You'd do it for Randolph Scott!"

The funeral itself went off more or less as planned the next afternoon. The embalmer did an excellent job and the suit and tie we picked out was a solid choice. There weren't many mourners, but truth be told I don't think any of us wanted many people there in the first place. My mom contacted my dad's last surviving sibling, Carolyn, to inform her of the funeral and she said, "I thought Danny had been dead for years."

Isaac and Kate were in attendance. As I mentioned, Chad couldn't be there, but sent a text saying, "Hey man, I'm thinking of you today. Your dad was always a nice guy to me." Sure enough, David and Lu Ann Cochran showed up right before the ceremony, having driven all the way from Henderson.

"Why, hello!" my mom exclaimed. "I had no idea you all were coming!"

David and Lu Ann consoled my mom before Lu Ann went over to the casket and remarked, "Danny still looks like such a young man."

Soon after, the minister started the ceremony, first playing "Against the Wind." Lu Ann was puzzled and turned to David to whisper, "Is that Bob Seger?" The speech itself was what we had agreed on, right down to the *Ride the High Country* reference. Then, as we agreed, "Turn the Page" played. It was an eerie note to end on, but I felt the song conveyed the message of the day well enough.

As the group of pallbearers loaded the casket, the grief hit me full-on. Suddenly I broke down in tears right in front of Isaac, Eric, and David. An embarrassing moment, but perhaps a long needed one. The twenty-two years since my dad's stroke hit me all at once and I needed to let out my grief. Frankly, I wish Eric would have also let out his, since he never seemed to let out any emotion of the sort. After a couple of minutes, I finished crying. I had gotten it out of my system. The past year had been full of awful mistakes, but foolish crypto decisions are only about money. This was real. This was family. This was what mattered.

Soon after, we loaded the coffin into the hearse and headed out to the same cemetery where Amanda's grandmother had recently been buried. My mom bought a dual plot, one spot for my dad and one for her. Amanda and I received a wind chime as a condolence gift, which still resides on our front porch today. None of my dad's old car salesmen buddies showed at all, almost echoing Willy Loman's funeral in *Death of a Salesman*. Even Bob Crenna, my dad's longtime friend from the car industry, didn't show. My mom later called him and asked why, only for Crenna to say, "Wait, was that yesterday? I lost all track of time. Sorry." I don't think my mom had much use for Crenna after those remarks. You can tell who really cares by who shows up at your funeral.

In the days following, I tried to understand why my dad ever bothered with renovating the old house in Henderson. I think deep down I understand his reasoning better now. By 1996, my dad was at his own crossroads in life, having burned most bridges with car dealers in Louisville. He saw inheriting the house in Henderson as a way out. A way back to a simpler and happier time for him, I suppose. Either that or a different type of unhappiness. He too wanted to leave Louisville, but at the end of the day, never could.

The BitConnect lawsuit nonsense dragged on for years, frankly to the point where I almost lost all interest in it. Occasionally Amanda would ask me what happened recently with the case, and I would call Jasper Ward. I rarely ever got a hold of him, so I mainly talked to Abigail Green. Since there were so many cases, my lawsuit was transferred down to Florida where the much bigger crypto law firm Silver Mueller took charge of all the cases. The case was an inconclusive mess, as trying to tie YouTube into the lawsuit went nowhere. In the wake of the BitConnect fiasco, YouTube and Facebook banned such overt promotional videos or ads for crypto investments.

Most of the main BitConnect promoters have been charged by the Securities and Exchange Commission for selling unlicensed securities, but I haven't heard much else about them since 2021. Are these guys mere con men? Perhaps. Or were they naïve fools used by the bigger players in BitConnect, ones who have never been found? Maybe multiple things can be true.

Zachary Coburn, the founder of EtherDelta, was also targeted by the SEC for running an unlicensed exchange. He was fined $300,000 without ever admitting or denying the findings, and I believe he sold off EtherDelta to someone overseas. I'm not sure what happened to the site, but it is now defunct.

I was sick of waiting for lawyers to remedy the situation. I looked online for updates on the case and saw the main American BitConnect promoter, Glenn Arcaro, had been arrested and was about to plead guilty to his role in BitConnect. I barely knew Arcaro from a couple of YouTube videos. I went to the FBI website and also the Southern California Department of Justice site and found a Victim Impact Statement and filled it out. Dina DeBoer handled my case with the DOJ and has been helpful explaining what needed to be done in order to be reimbursed.

On January 30, 2023, I got an email after one last Arcaro hearing informing me I was going to be reimbursed $5,219. The email said the district court could take several months to figure out how to disperse the twenty-one million dollars seized from Arcaro, since there were still victims coming forward with claims. As of this writing, I am still waiting for the reimbursement check to arrive. Justice is out there; sometimes you have to look for it.

There is a constant saying in crypto: "Don't invest what you cannot afford to lose." It strikes me as such a bizarre statement, one giving carte blanche to all sorts of rug pulls, exit scams, and general con artist behavior. We haven't been forced onto the street over my ill- advised attempts to become the king of crypto, but there is no justification for perpetuating a scam. Eventually, I will get that $5,219 back, but as of now, I am still waiting. (Update: The U.S. Treasury check arrived on 10-31-23). I still need to figure out a way to pay back my mom, however. I heard OlympusDAO is a promising crypto project. Just kidding.

CHAPTER 18

THE PRAIRIE VILLAGE "ALL STARS"

July 2022. In the years since I played youth baseball, the rise of travel teams has seriously harmed leagues around the country. Instead of playing in a local recreation league, the best baseball players often try out for travel teams and often go out of town (even the state) for weekend tournaments. This situation applies to coaches as well, with the better youth baseball coaches now going into travel ball. My old league, Beechmont, is a shell of what it used to be and is hardly alone in this regard.

Travel team baseball is quite expensive for parents. Not only does a kid need a regulation USSSA bat, which cost $200-$300, but the fees associated with travel ball can run into the thousands each year. Those fee numbers are sheer madness to me, who was used to recreation leagues having the top talent to go along with the guys just happy to be there. There are some kids who play both travel ball and rec league baseball, with leagues having to adjust schedules due to travel tournaments. Amanda and I have never steered Andrew toward travel team baseball due to the expense involved and because he doesn't have that level of commitment to the game. Instead, Andrew has played in the Prairie Village Babe Ruth League.

I have long considered Prairie Village a joke, but it's about five minutes from my house and Andrew has played there since Tee Ball. PV was a joke when I played, and I figured they would be a joke now. Andrew's games over the past two years in the 9–10 division have largely been horrid experiences, a bunch of undertrained boys facing lousy pitching in 19–18 walk fests.

The longer I watch Andrew play youth baseball, the more disenchanted I become. I see nonsense that wouldn't have been tolerated when I played. Kids running to second base after a walk and being allowed to do so. Runners on third racing halfway down the line after every pitch, with the pitcher rushing back to the mound to keep the runner from moving. I've seen teams forfeit games after only six players showed up. The white trash nature of the coaches is especially troubling. I have witnessed opposing coaches argue with teenage umpires, intimidating these kids into overturning calls.

In 2021, Andrew played for Sherman Watkins's Diamondbacks team and played terribly. Sherman himself is a nice enough guy and has a prosthetic leg much like Amanda, but he struck me as someone barely in charge of his own team, content with letting his assistants run roughshod. Sherman liked Andrew well enough, but the main assistants didn't. Subsequently, Andrew was buried at the end of the bench and didn't get a single hit that season.

Andrew wanted to quit playing, but we talked him into trying one more season. Since I didn't want him anywhere near the Diamondbacks again, we had him try out for other coaches. To my bewilderment, his coach ended up being one Ava Stone. At first, I was bewildered at the idea of a woman coaching a boys baseball team, but Andrew enjoyed playing for her. I discerned hostility towards Ava from certain coaches. Her arguments with the Cubs' coaches (including the aforementioned Josh Robinson incident) during games and even over who had the field for practice echoed a certain macho sexism. Once I moved past my own initial doubts, I saw the potential in the team. Talentwise it was easily the best team Andrew had been on.

Almost overnight, Andrew reverted back to his 2020 form as an eight-year-old, immediately getting hit after hit. Andrew would have been an All-Star in 2020, but there were no All-Star games due to Covid-19. He has never had a consistent field position, going from right field to shortstop, with some occasional left field or even third thrown in. This was one of my problems with Ava as a coach. She put kids all over the place instead of letting them focus on one position.

Toward the end of the season, I wondered if Andrew was going to be a candidate for the All-Star team. Prairie Village had both a nine- and ten-year-old team, so half the league was on some version of an All-Star team. The league barely had enough talent for one team. Sherman was set to coach this team due to the Diamondbacks winning the league championship over our Red Sox, mainly because of a couple of victories when we faced them missing key players. I felt they were fraudulent, though, relying on a few hitters with everyone else being told to keep the bats on their shoulders to draw walks.

I knew this team was going to be bad, even though Sherman insisted otherwise. When Sherman showed me the roster, I asked him, "Aside from Brandon Baylor [assistant coach Bobby Baylor's son], where is the pitching here?" In fact, I didn't see much of anything. No pitching, not much hitting, and guys stacked three deep at certain positions without anyone at other positions.

Andrew was one of the last kids to make the team as an alternate, receiving two coaches votes out of four. I knew the Cubs' coach wouldn't vote for him, but I was surprised to find out Rob Brewer didn't vote for Andrew either. I've known Rob on and off since 1987 when we played on Larry Kirby's team at Beechmont three different years. I thought Rob would pick Andrew for his own team, but he didn't. Rob's Reds ended up being a one-win disaster, though, so Andrew dodged that bullet.

The coaching staff had zero clue, and they took everything out on the boys. We planned to use the Fern Creek tournament, now known as the Firecracker tourney, to see what we had. At the first practice, they insisted those who showed up to practice would be the kids getting the playing time and if you didn't show up then you could expect to sit. That was a bold-faced lie. We never missed a single practice, yet Andrew received little playing time.

One of the main problems the coaches had was the presumption all these boys could hit, despite most regular season games being absurd walk-a-thons. This became a problem at Fern Creek, where the team managed to score a grand total of six runs over three games while giving up thirty-six. At any one point, I was never sure what sort of hitting philosophy the coaches were teaching. Were the kids supposed to be aggressive? Should they try to draw as many walks as possible? Something in between? No one was ever sure.

Fern Creek was not the same ballpark I remembered. The league had no bleachers since they never brought them back after the pandemic. Everyone had to bring their own lawn chairs. Further, the bathrooms were being renovated, so only porta-potties could be used around the ballpark. Half the scoreboards weren't working either. Why did they bother to host a tournament?

During the Fern Creek tourney, I made up with Josh Robinson, the Cubs' first base coach and the 2002 Valley Sports World Champion I argued with during the regular season. I approached him while he was nursing an injured knee in his lawn chair.

"Hey, I just wanted to apologize for that blowup a couple of months back," I said. "The entire thing was stupid and should have never happened."

"Water under the bridge as far as I'm concerned," he replied.

Josh's son, Craig, made the team, at least for a while until Josh had to have knee surgery. Craig was one of the few highlights of this Fern Creek tourney, since he had a couple of hits and made a nice catch in the outfield. Robinson's text to the group was bizarre, though, noting his surgery for a torn meniscus but also said, "Craig doesn't want to play on the team anymore." Craig wasn't the only one to quit. Roster turnover became a trademark of this team.

Andrew barely got any playing time at Fern Creek. He didn't play in the field or bat vs. West Louisville, had one at bat vs. Blue Lick and walked on four pitches, then got another walk and played a little in left field vs. Germantown. Given the overall pathetic lack of hitting, I couldn't help but wonder why they didn't use Andrew more. These boys were so used to drawing walks they didn't know how to hit serious pitching.

Watching the practices before the district tournament made me start to question things. Bobby and Brandon Baylor skipped some practices. Brandon had a broken catching hand and Sherman didn't want him playing due to liability concerns. What made things worse was Bobby acted like a lunatic in practice when he was around, barking and yelling at kids for any fielding error, making boys run laps on hot summer evenings, even made Brandon do twenty-five pushups *on a broken hand*. One of the other coaches, Terry Halliwell, was on the Prairie Village board and lectured Bobby on this crazy behavior. I never quite understood Terry being a coach on this team since his son was on the 9U team.

Speaking of the 9U team, Ava Stone had to coach that misbegotten group and things went south in a hurry. Having seen the roster, the only serious talent on it was from our Red Sox team, which frankly made me wish some of those guys were on the 10U team. The rest of the kids I either didn't know or knew sucked, so I wasn't surprised when they too went winless and were shellacked at Fern Creek.

Ava inexplicably used two ten-year-old kids in the district tourney, so they would have had to forfeit those games if they had won any of them. Sometimes the team practiced on another field while Andrew's team was practicing, and I noticed fewer and fewer kids showing up. As Terry mentioned, there had been parent complaints that Ava wasn't developing talent, favored her own players, and had boys playing entirely new positions. I still don't understand why she was so desperate as to put a couple of ten-year-olds on the team.

One of these kids, Brensen, played on Andrew's team, so Ava had to know his age. Brensen would hardly move the needle, so I wondered why she'd even bothered with this subterfuge. Brensen moved over to the 10U team, and the entire coaching staff loved the kid's effort, even starting him on occasion.

During the build for the district tourney, Sherman let loose on some bizarre personal problems. I had noticed his wife, Christy, hadn't been around as much this season but didn't really ask about it. As it turned out, she had fallen in love with an online scammer who was going around social media impersonating WWE star Seth Rollins, conning gullible fans into giving him money. Christy had been aiding this guy with his scams by opening various bank accounts. Eventually, a detective showed up at their house wanting to talk to her. Even after being found out, she told Sherman she would rather be with "Rollins" than him. Add in Sherman's various Covid-related health problems over the past year and he seemed preoccupied with other things.

The district tourney was held at West Louisville's ballpark in Shawnee Park. For those from Louisville, that statement no doubt brought a "WTF?" reaction. Who in their right mind would schedule a major tournament in the west end? Early on when Sherman mentioned the district tourney would be in West Louisville, I responded, "No, really. Where is the actual tourney being held?" No one wanted to go down there, especially for an 8:00 p.m. game. Several parents and coaches openly talked of carrying a firearm, which I found a little ridiculous.

When we arrived at the ballpark, there were already people waving at us not to park in the lot, noting six people had already had their cars broken into. The situation became so ridiculous that most people moved their cars to the open lawn area near the field, which required jumping the curb on the street to do so.

PV had to play West Louisville at their place in the first round. I wasn't ultra-impressed with them the first time, feeling our hitters didn't try to work any at bats or make the pitcher work at all, swinging at anything and making this kid into the second coming of Bob Gibson. Sure enough, the guys were more patient, and we jumped out to a solid 7–4 lead. Bobby was ejected by the ump for arguing about whether West Louisville could pinch hit for their Designated Hitter, and he went off like a nut, cussing this guy out. I was shocked he didn't let some racial epithets fly at the African American ump or the all Black

West Louisville team. Bobby had a point, and the ump apologized the next day for the call itself. This sort of lunacy was still embarrassing to be around, though. Between feeling embarrassed and ill at ease due to being in Shawnee Park late at night, the environment was the most unsettling I've ever been around for a youth baseball game.

Regardless of his hand, Brandon was the team's one feasible pitcher and once he left games, things went south in a hurry. He left the West Louisville game up 7–4 and the rest of the way we were outscored 20 to 0, losing 24–7. Andrew was the only player on the team who didn't get any sort of playing time. Even Brensen, who had joined the team a week earlier, got into the game and had one at bat while Andrew sat. I didn't even want to go back for the next game, but why would I? We had to go down to the ghetto, risk our car being stolen or broken into, watch horrific baseball, and Andrew didn't even get to play. Who would want more of this? The next day, Amanda talked to Sherman, asking why Andrew received zero playing time. Better she talk to him than me. I was ready to tell Sherman to go to hell.

Sherman agreed with Amanda and also revealed to us due to some sort of fluke with teams in the rest of the state, everyone from our district would make the state tourney at Fairdale. He should have mentioned this announcement to the parents freaking out over losing one more game and being eliminated. The decision rendered the district tourney pointless, though.

Overall, the West Louisville tourney was a rain-plagued fiasco. The first game was originally rained out. The second game was rained out. Finally, the entire bracket was changed and instead of being in the loser's bracket and facing Fairdale, we had a rematch with German-town, who crushed us 16–1 at Fern Creek. The Saturday game was rained out after two innings. What made matters worse was we all got sick, I'm sure due to hanging around in the rain.

Andrew was the DH in the Germantown game, hitting dead last in the lineup of course, and walked all three times. Germantown played without their two top pitchers, a couple of ringers they brought in from Indianapolis. Somehow this didn't seem quite fair to me, these out-of-state guys playing here, but what can you do? I started feeling sad for Andrew after this game, when I asked him why he seemed so tentative to do anything at the plate. He told me, "I'm afraid if I even strike out one time, they will never play me again."

Another kid quit/was thrown off the team during this district tourney. Tyler Harper's dad wasn't on the group meet app, so Sherman sometimes forgot to send him messages about games. He didn't know to show up for the rescheduled Saturday game, then didn't show up at all for the Sunday continuation of it. He wouldn't have been in the lineup since the lineup card had already been turned in. Still, I thought losing him was a bad move. Tyler Harper was a serious athlete who could glide around the bases. Personally, I would have made another call to his dad, but Sherman kicked him off the team instead.

As far as the game itself is concerned, Brandon had to be removed after hitting his pitch count and the guys that came in for relief turned a 9–9 tie into a 21–10 beating. I thought things were looking up, though. The team needed someone else to pitch besides Brandon. Either way, we now headed to the state tournament, even though we had gone a combined 0–5 and been ten runned in four of those games.

As Andrew's team prepared for the state tournament, the coaches had largely given up on trying to make the team any better. Given the lack of hitting in the offense, I'm still baffled as to why the coaches didn't practice batting more often. Many of the practices consisted of lining up boys in the field and having everyone do one or two tasks. Infielders took grounders and threw to first, while outfielders shagged flies. There was no situational awareness being practiced in a way that made sense, no work on our horrendous base running, not much of anything. At times the weather was too hot to practice much and JCPS forbade anything on school grounds, adding to the team's woes.

I felt the key to any chance the team had at the state tournament rested with Ace Jackman. Ace was the most talented player in the 9–10 league at Prairie Village. He was the closest thing the league had to a five-tool player, although no one at this level is hitting for power. Ace could hit the ball hard, was a quick runner, and had a rocket for an arm. Ace had the problem of being totally undisciplined, someone who was the epitome of a player who kept both teams in the game. In one inning, Ace might drive in two runs with a triple, then throw the ball away trying to pick a runner off third. Or Ace might throw out a runner trying to steal second, but then make a baserunning mistake to take us out of an inning. He was also flat-out allergic to walks, swinging at any crazy pitch.

Ace was tantalizing for any manager to use as a pitcher due to his arm and velocity, but he couldn't get the ball over the plate with any regularity. Ava tried pitching him a few times in relief during the season, with questionable results. The only time Ace started was a game we badly needed against the Diamondbacks where he walked everyone again, digging a 5–1 hole after one inning. As Ace's grandpa said, "Ace does *not* need to be pitching."

I didn't quite know what other options we had other than Brandon. Two other pitchers were outscored a combined 32–1 in West Louisville when they came in to pitch relief. Ace came in during garbage time vs. Germantown and retired the last batter easily, so I thought he might be a decent idea to come in after Brandon for relief. I even told Sherman as much.

The state tournament at Fairdale didn't seem much like a state event, since no one from outside the Louisville area competed in it, with Mt. Washington being the lone team from outside Jefferson County participating (from nearby Bullitt County). We were assigned to Pool B along with my old league, Beechmont, and St. Matthews.

Once again Andrew was not in the lineup at all. Bobby had talked to Sherman and convinced him to start Ace as pitcher, with Brandon catching. I already knew Ace was a disaster as a starting pitcher since he needed to be in the flow of the game. Shockingly, we jumped out 7–0 on a lousy opponent in Beechmont, only to then have Ace not be able to get out of the first inning. Brandon immediately came in to relieve, but he too was ineffective. By the time the smoke cleared, Beechmont put up twelve runs in one inning.

I still felt awful and had to blow my nose repeatedly, but I never tested positive for Covid. After a point, I stopped caring and quit watching, preferring to watch some of the other games on the bigger field. The final score ended up being 19–7, repeating a bad pattern. We could hit early on, but then the other team would put in a different pitcher and we stopped hitting. Or we would stay close until the relief pitching coughed up the lead. Once again, the game turned into our coaches ranting about this rule or that rule to the ump, to the point where the ump had to threaten to eject all the coaches.

One thing that made these tourneys all the worse was having to pay for admission. We dropped about $30 at Fern Creek, another $20 at West Louisville, and $36 at Fairdale. That's $86 total to watch some truly horrible baseball in which Andrew barely played. We also had to sell ten raffle tickets for the All Stars, after selling six for regular season games. We managed to find enough people to sell ten raffle tickets, but several other people didn't and handed over $100 for those tickets. Things like this made me realize the entire thing was a scam. By having two All Star teams at the 9–10 level, they made twice the money from those raffle tickets. Who cared if the on-field product was awful if you're raking in this much jack?

Around this point I was looking to get away from this whole disaster of an All-Star experience. I figured we'd go to Fern Creek, play a few games, lose twice, and be done. But this was dragging on and on with these kids becoming more and more emotionally beaten up by these losses. This team didn't belong in a state tourney and frankly I was offended they were gifted a free pass to it. I never got near a state tournament when I played. Everyone wanted their little participation trophy, I suppose.

The next day Amanda once again texted Sherman asking whether Andrew was going to be in the lineup vs. St. Matthews that night. Sherman said he was listed again as the DH, but there was a whole lot more. Bobby quit after the Beechmont game and took Brandon with him. Bobby wasn't a major loss, but Brandon was. I didn't know the details, other than Bobby was offended at something a parent said to Brandon after the game.

The St. Matthews game was of course a total fiasco, but in this case, mainly because St. Matthews was easily the best team in the tournament. The score was 21–0 and they were ferocious. The catcher took offense to us having any baserunners, throwing out the leadoff hitter at second after a walk and picking off our only other runner. Andrew was batting during the latter, so he technically didn't make an out. The ump called mercy after three innings. For the tourney, St. Matthews scored a total of seventy-seven runs and gave up three.

After this game, Sherman jumped on the group meet and did an about-face, saying the result had been his fault and he was going to let Bobby and Terry do the lineup for the next day's elimination game vs. Jeffersontown. He also said we needed Brandon and Bobby back if we were going to win. Enough was enough. I couldn't believe Sherman would let these guys quit and come back after one day, especially after kicking Tyler Harper off the team for missing a game.

I took to the group meet and let loose. "This is Brian. As far as I'm concerned, those guys quit on this team and when you do that you have no further say in terms of planning a lineup or in terms of playing time."

Terry fired back saying I didn't know the full story, and then Bobby told the full story. A parent upset Brandon after the Beechmont game saying he was "a no-talent fat boy who wasn't a serious All Star and only got playing time because his dad was a coach." Brandon didn't even want to play baseball anymore and Bobby started talking about the team not being a "safe space." Bobby said they wouldn't be back. As far as I was concerned, good riddance. The vitriol directed toward Brandon made little sense given his gutsy effort with the bad hand. He was the closest thing to a top pitcher and hitter on the league champions.

I will admit to the self-serving motivation behind my text. I realized someone on the coaching staff had a problem with Andrew and didn't want him to play. This situation seemed like retaliation for leaving the Diamondbacks after last season. Sherman vouched for Andrew, so I don't think he was the problem. The other coaches didn't know

Andrew, so that left Bobby as the coach who made sure he didn't get off the bench. Andrew went from being a confident player to once again being the "deer in the headlights" kid scared to do anything from the previous year. They messed with his head so badly to the point where he didn't even know which bat to use when he went to the plate, since his bat he used so well that year was "too big for such a small kid."

The tournament came down to one final game, an elimination round vs. Jeffersontown. The team had ten boys left, but instead of batting everyone 1–10, which was allowed, they went 1–9 yet again and had Andrew sub RF with Donnie Brewer (Rob's son, who Sherman saw nothing in). Even to the last they had to be petty pricks.

The game was seemingly another in a long line of beatings. J-Town, while not a good team whatsoever, jumped out 13–1 after four innings and the game looked all but over. Andrew finally struck out in his first at bat. It was the only out he made the entire All-Star season. Sure enough, the next inning I looked out to see Donnie playing right field. Andrew was right all along. One strikeout and they pulled him.

J-Town took out their solid starting pitcher going into the fifth. The backup pitchers, to be blunt, were horrid. The score suddenly went from 13–1 to 13–6 and we had bases loaded with no outs. This being the Prairie Village 10U team, we managed to screw up. Donnie was now up instead of Andrew and the count was 2–2. The scoreboard looked wrong to me and said 3–2 was the count. The next pitch was a ball. The baserunners casually jogged to the next base, but the home ump meekly said, "Count is full now."

The catcher tagged the runner going home and then threw to second and tagged another runner. One strike later and the inning was over. The players and coaches should always be aware of the count regardless of the scoreboard, but this was clearly a scorer error and the home plate ump needed to call time and have them fix the scoreboard and allow the runners to return to their bases. He didn't, though, and we got the shaft. For once, the coaches didn't even make that much of a stir.

J-Town added insurance runs in the sixth to make the score 16–6.

But in the bottom of the inning, they still had the same hideous pitchers, and once again we started putting up runs. Donnie was lifting again after lollygagging in the field and Andrew was back in the lineup. Sure enough, Andrew hit one last time and I have never felt more anxious about an at bat. I didn't want him to be the last out of the entire season the way I was in the 1991 playoff game. By now, I realized Andrew had lost all confidence in hitting and making contact, so I was hoping for a walk. He took a couple of decent pitches, ones barely low or slightly high, and drew a two out walk. I exhaled. Ace batted next and lined out to center to end the game. Final score, 16–11.

Andrew had one of the strangest stats lines I've ever seen. He was 0–1 with a .000 batting average, but his on base percentage was .889. He walked eight of nine times and may well have had the highest OBP on the team. What's remarkably terrible was he never scored a single time. Despite hitting last and walking incessantly, none of the guys at the top of the order ever knocked him in.

In the last postgame team meeting, Terry asked all the kids what they had learned during the All-Star season. I was amused at Andrew's response: "Nothing." What more needed to be said?

I talked to Brensen's mom, who by now loathed Ava over the entire 9U situation, and said, "Brensen made the most of this opportunity. He played hard out there, probably because he wasn't as mentally beaten down as these other kids." She nodded in agreement.

After this All-Star fiasco, we were done with Prairie Village. Sherman talked of trying to keep this group together as an 11U travel team next year, and quite frankly didn't interest me. Ava later texted saying she was moving over to Valley Sports in the fall. After the entire 9U debacle, I don't see how she could ever show her face again at Prairie Village. Given what happened with that team, I must question whether I want Andrew playing for her again. The accusations of dishonesty made me look at other events during the season, such as the double booking of the field for practice that led to animosity with the Cubs (their coach accused Ava of crossing them out on the signup sheet).

I don't know where Prairie Village goes from here. Only seven kids signed up for 11–12 Fall Ball. We will give Valley Sports a shot next year and hopefully Andrew can find a coach who will maximize what he can do as a player and help him learn a few things. Could Andrew help them get back to the Little League World Series, which Valley Sports won in 2002? Probably not. But I doubt a new league could possibly be worse than what has been going on at Prairie Village over the past few years.

AFTERWORD

Andrew switched over to Valley Sports for the 2023 season, along with nearly everyone else from Prairie Village's All Star Team who didn't make a travel team. Of course, he struggled moving into the 11–12 division, in part because Valley Sports allows kids thirteen years old to play with the younger kids. Andrew is now going to Farnsley Middle School, and hopefully his experiences there will be better than my experiences at Noe.

Amanda is still plugging away at Rutherford Elementary but has wanted to transfer out for years. She hasn't had the right opportunity, and Human Resources at JCPS is a disaster in terms of how they handle transfers. She should have had a Fairdale computer lab job, but a mix-up with her certification expiring led to the system kicking out her application. JCPS strikes me as a dysfunctional district these days.

Amanda takes Andrew to Valley View on Sundays, but I still stay home. She mainly participates in her Sunday School life group and not the actual church service itself, while Andrew heads to a kid's class. I am not an atheist, but I have never been interested in organized religion and church. This is a difference we've learned to live with over the years.

Isaac and Kate now have a three-year-old named Gabriel. Isaac is still on disability for his epileptic fits as far as I know. Kate works from home doing online customer service work. Isaac's mom, Bonnie, lives with them. They live fairly close to me, right off Johnsontown Road. Isaac's older daughter, Megan, lives with her mother in Toledo. I still try to invite Isaac over for wrestling PPVs, but with a small child at home, he hasn't had as much time.

Chad is now working in the mortgage industry but isn't thrilled with doing so anymore since banks have started offering better deals than what his mortgage company can afford. He and Harley have two children, Oliver and Jacqueline. I still talk to Chad on the phone from time to time, but we haven't gotten together since before the pandemic. In fact, the last time we saw each other may well have been when he helped refinance our mortgage. Maybe we will see each other again sometime soon.

My mom is still with us, although I can't say she is in great health. Sometimes she has the same trouble eating and coughing that my dad had in 2001. Eric still lives with her, and over time has become even more of a recluse. He isn't showering regularly anymore and has never had a job even though he's almost thirty-four years old. I don't know what will become of him if my mom dies or has to enter a nursing home. Eric is quite intelligent, but he's never had much of a chance in life. Living with ailing parents for most of his life has left him quite broken, I think.

I was saddened to hear Jeremy Stigler died of a heart attack on August 17, 2023. He was forty-three. While we hadn't stayed in touch over the years, he was one of my best friends from childhood. I shared the Beechmont story with him after our chance meeting at Tire Discounters, and I saw him from time to time in the car rider line at Stonestreet Elementary since his son had started kindergarten there.

As for myself, well, that's more complicated. I had long since stopped caring about subbing for JCPS by the time the pandemic hit. After in-person school resumed, Andrew's morning Child Enrichment Program was cancelled at Stonestreet, so I took Andrew to school and picked him up, which made subbing all but impossible. The last straw was when I applied for a social studies job at Manual, and despite being one of their preferred subs for years, wasn't granted so much as an interview. After that slight, I decided to quit. I cashed out of the Teachers Retirement System and didn't look back. I never figured out how to crack the code with Manual, neither as a student thirty years ago when I applied or trying to teach at the school full time in recent years.

While I sold the Canon XL2 years ago to someone on Amazon, I still occasionally flirt with the idea of entering screenplay contests or sending out letters of inquiry to various producers and agents who accept unsolicited submissions. I don't have any serious notion of selling a script, but film is one dream I can't ever let die entirely.

Amanda and I still talk about trying to move out of Louisville. We have looked at homes outside of Jefferson County in Bullitt County or Oldham County, but given the current home prices and interest rates, moving isn't financially viable. In some ways I feel similar to how my dad felt by the time he hit his 40s, and as I creep nearer to my 46th birthday (the age when he had the stroke), the more I understand him. I just need to get my blood pressure checked more often.

Sometimes on weekends we go to eat at Outback off Fern Valley Road, which is quite close to Tanglewood. As such, we drive by the remnants of the old Holiday Inn. Most of the Fern Valley Road exit off I-65 is run-down and eerie. The powers that be in the city have tried hard over the past twenty years to renew downtown Louisville, and of course there's always new construction farther out in the county.

But everything else? The Louisville I grew up in? The Louisville of Denny Crum, Louisville Gardens, Crawford Gym, and old Cardinal Stadium? The Louisville of the '80s and '90s? It doesn't really exist anymore. Most of it has faded away with the passage of time. Louisville is very much a city where if you're from here, you know there is a bigger world out there, but to access the bigger world you need to move somewhere else. To someone like my dad from small town Kentucky, Louisville *was* that bigger world.

One of my last sub jobs was a long-term assignment at Manual doing online Non Traditional Instruction (NTI), right before in-person classes resumed in March 2021. During my weeks subbing journalism, a student at Manual committed suicide. I knew him a little bit from subbing a couple of his classes the previous year, and I let the students grieve his loss. I shared this statement with some of the seniors at the time: "I know you're upset but listen to me. There is nothing in high school, or any other time, worth killing yourself over. Maybe yesterday wasn't a very good day. Maybe today hasn't been much better. But you know what? Maybe tomorrow will be better. All you have to do is wake up in the morning and find out."

Perhaps there has to be a little rain sometime, but it certainly can't rain all the time. I know as much because I saw *The Crow* with my dad at River Falls Mall on May 15th, 1994.

ABOUT THE AUTHOR

Brian Paige is an author who lives in Louisville, Kentucky, with his wife, Amanda, and son, Andrew. He is a 2001 graduate of the University of Louisville with a Bachelor of Arts in Communications, 2011 U of L graduate with a Master of Arts in Communication, and 2016 graduate of the University of the Cumberlands with a Master of Arts in Teaching in secondary social studies. He also has a self-produced album under the name Demo, *Sonic Screamer*.